INDONESIAN CUISINE
"Selamat Makan"

First published in 1998 by
Pulido Publications Inc.
7645 E. Evans Rd. Suite 6
Scottsdale, AZ. 85260
888-626-0944

ISBN # 0-9663787-0-9

Printed and Bound in the U.S.A.

INDONESIAN CUISINE
"Selamat Makan"

By Esly van de Weerdt-Schieffelers

Photography & Food Styling
Ingram * Twombly

Editor
Patrica Tierney - Cascone

Book & Cover Design
Square One Design Inc.

Publisher
Pulido Publications Inc.

ACKNOWLEDGMENTS

I would like to dedicate this book to the memory of my Indonesian grandmother, Sapae Schieffelers. It was her tremendous talents as a cook and her fierce dedication to her family that inspired me to strive to preserve her legacy.

I would also like to extend my thanks to my children, Francisca and Brian Pulido, who have helped me fulfill my life-long dream - publishing this cookbook.

Esly in the arm of her mother

To my readers:

I was born in 1930 in the town of Semarang. Semarang is located on the island of Java in Indonesia. I lived there for a few years before moving to Malang, also located on Java.

In 1937 I had the wonderful fortune of taking a world-wide tour with my family. We departed by boat, visiting Japan, China, Hawaii and finally reached the west coast of America. Once in America, we toured Yellow Stone Park, the Rocky Mountains, Hollywood, San Francisco and other parts of California. From there we went to Chicago where we visited the large slaughter houses. I was only seven years old at the time, and I ran out of there, frightened. It was nothing for a child to see. From Chicago we went by train, to New York City. I was lost in the bustling crowd there for a while, but thankfully, I eventually found my family. From New York we sailed to the Netherlands and settled down there. In total, it was a three-month journey. How wonderful!

In 1940, World War II began. After five long years of extremely difficult times, life changed for the better. Peace and freedom were given to us by the Canadian and American Soldiers. I remain thankful and gracious for that gift of freedom. Love, life and freedom can be taken away tomorrow. I take nothing for granted anymore. I'm just thankful to be alive.

In 1950, I was married. My husband, Frans, and I had five children. Two boys and three girls. In 1968 my family and I moved to the United States. Sadly, I became a widow in 1989. All of my children are either married or on their own. The nest is now empty. But it has provided me with the time to write this cookbook.

My hope is that my family - children and grand children - will enjoy this cookbook and remember, fondly, the gatherings and celebrations of holidays and birthdays and that they do this with joy in their hearts.

Esly at play

FORWARD

It sometimes takes only one person in your life who's influence helps you to become the person you are today. For me, that person is my Indonesian grandmother, Sapae Schieffelers. It was she who taught me to respect and love myself first. But, also to respect every living and growing thing on earth - because it is all created by the "spirit".

The memories I have of my grandmother are tender ones. Family gatherings were infrequent. My grandmother lived 800 miles away from us. But the memories are vivid and happy ones. As a child, my

Esly with her mother & grandmother Sapae Schieffelers

favorite spot was in my grandmother's garden. She had a fountain that was so large you could stand under it and take a shower. The garden was filled with flowers, herbs and talking and singing birds. One of these birds was able to perfectly mimic my grandmother's voice calling the maid. The maid came many times to the garden, only to find the bird staring smugly at her. She was not pleased, to say the least.

The people who live in the villages that make up a large part of Indonesia are generally poor. The act of sitting down for a meal is a pleasurable event. It is a time where family gathers. All of the female members of the family contribute in some way to the preparation of the meal. It is this way, that recipes and the art of cooking are handed down from one family to the next.

Despite the unfortunate poverty that is so prevalent in most of these villages, Indonesia itself is rich in natural resources. Exported agricultural products include palm oil, coffee, tea, cocoa, tobacco, sugar and spices. The native cuisine is representative of this abundance. Most every dish contains intense flavor, created by the science of combining just the right amount of spice in ratio to vegetables and meats. Texture is another important attribute of their food. Coconut, fruit, peanuts and other assorted nuts are commonly used. It is an earthy cuisine, taking the best of nature, combining it in just the right way, resulting in an unforgettable meal.

The many recipes contained within the pages of this book are the very ones that my grandmother prepared for her family over 60 years ago. Many of the recipes were jotted down without measurement. Over the years I have adjusted them to my family and mine's tastes. There is a possibility that you may want to use more or less of certain ingredients. The trick with Indonesian cooking is that no two cooks' dishes are the same. Everyone has their own tastes and preferences. Once you understand the techniques involved in cooking the Indonesian way, it will be easier for you to decide what should be adjusted.

I hope you find the recipes contained in this book as delicious and joyful as my family and I have. Selamat Makan, (enjoy your meal).

TABLE OF CONTENTS

Diagram represents photo on previous page

RICE TABLE (DE RYSTTAFEL)

1. Spicy Bamboo Shoot Relish	8. Rice
2. Sautéed Chicken in a Ginger Sauce	9. Ordinary Cucumber Salad
3. Pork Satay	10. Omelet with Chicken Livers
4. Pork in Kecap Sauce	11. Krupuk
5. Curried Java Soup	12. Sambal Ulek
6. Spiced Shredded Coconut with Peanuts	13. Plain Sliced Cucumbers
7. Fish in a Hot Paprika Sauce	14. Sambal Ulek

RICE TABLE
(DE RYSTTAFEL)

The rice table (or De Rysttafel) is a buffet-type of menu with the rice being the main dish and many side dishes to compliment it. The host and/or cook usually chooses dishes which will suit a variety of tastes and likes, such as a fair representation of various meats; chicken, beef, pork and fish, as well as an offering of spicy and non-spicy dishes accompanied by an abundant assortment of vegetables.

In the Indonesian culture, when an important guest is invited to dinner, the more food that is presented is the host's way of conveying a compliment; showing how distinguished or "special" their dinner guest is. Essentially, the more food that is presented, the more important the guest is.

When the rice table is used for special occasions, such as weddings or holidays, the menu can consist of as many as twenty side dishes with the rice, of course, being the main dish.

The recipes contained within this chapter represent what I would normally serve to guests in my home. However, any additions or changes you may want to make are perfectly acceptable.

Tumis Rebung
SPICY BAMBOO SHOOT RELISH

Chef's Notes:
Serve this relish with white rice, krupuk, your choice of chicken dish, salad and omelets.

Dish #1

1 can	Unsalted bamboo shoots, drained
1	Red chilie, unseeded and minced
2	Green chilies, unseeded and minced
1	Clove garlic, minced
2-3	Scallions, minced
11/2 tbsp	Butter
1/2 tsp	Salt
1/2 tsp	Shrimp paste (trassi)
1/2 tsp	Tamarind (asam)
1/2 inch	Laos or 1/2 tsp powder
2	Small bay leaves (daun salam)
1 cup	Hot Water
Dash	Sugar
8 oz	Coconut Milk

❁ To prepare, cut drained bamboo shoots into 1-inch pieces. Place bamboo shoots in pan with enough water to cover and boil for 8 minutes. Drain and set aside. In wok, set on medium heat, sauté the red and green chilies, garlic and scallions in butter for 2-3 minutes. Add salt, shrimp paste, tamarind, laos and bay leaves and continue simmering until scallions become light brown in color. Add hot water and bamboo shoots and simmer 2-3 minutes. Add sugar and coconut milk and simmer, uncovered, for 3 minutes. Add additional hot water as necessary to maintain consistent fluid level.

Ajam Goreng and Jahe Sauce
SAUTÉED CHICKEN IN A GINGER SAUCE

Chef's Notes:
*The ginger sauce should be served separately,
so that your guests can help themselves.
Serve with white rice and a vegetable soup.*

Dish #2

1	Whole chicken
	Salted water
3	Scallions
1 tsp	Coriander seed
	Salt, to taste
	Pepper, to taste
2 tbsp	Flour
8 oz	Coconut milk
	Butter or oil

Ginger Sauce:

2 cups	Hot water
2	Red chilies, unseeded and minced
1/4 tsp	Salt
1 tbsp	Vinegar
1/2 Cup	Java Sugar
1 tsp	Ginger powder (jahe)
2 tbsp	Flour
	Water

❀ Cut chicken into small pieces (about 2 inches). Boil chicken in salted water until done. Set aside. In bowl, combine scallions, coriander seed, salt, pepper, flour and coconut milk. Dip the chicken pieces in this mixture and using a wok, sauté in butter (or oil) until golden brown.

❀ *To prepare the ginger sauce:* bring 2 cups of water to a boil. Add red chilies, salt, vinegar, java sugar and ginger. Let simmer a few minutes. Make a flour paste by adding enough water to 2 tbsp of flour. Add the flour paste and let simmer a few more minutes. Pour the ginger sauce into a separate serving bowl and keep hot.

Satay Babi, I
PORK SATAY

Chef's Notes:
I prefer to marinate a day in advance, with or without the meat being skewered. When barbecuing, be careful not to use too hot of a fire. The meat will burn on the outside and the inside will be too raw. Keep one skewer to be used to test the doneness of the meat, periodically.

Dish #3

16 oz	Pork
3	Cloves garlic, minced and crushed
3	Scallions, minced and crushed
1/2 tsp	Salt
1 tbsp	Java sugar (gula-jawa)
1/2 tsp	Coriander (ketumbar), crushed
1/2 tsp	Ginger powder (jahe)
1/2 tbsp	Tamarind (asam) mixed w/enough water to form a paste (or can use tamarind jelly)
2 tbsp	Butter
3 tbsp	Kecap manis (sweet soy sauce)
1/2 tbsp	Lemon Juice
	Skewers (small wooden kind, usually sold 100 per bag)

❋ Slice meat into 1-inch cubes, set aside. In a ceramic or glass bowl, combine the garlic and scallions. To this add: Salt, java sugar, coriander seed, ginger and tamarind.

❋ In a separate pan, melt butter then remove from heat. To this add Kecap manis and lemon juice. Combine both mixtures in the glass or ceramic bowl, mixing thoroughly. Add the meat cubes, stir. Cover and let marinate in refrigerator for at least 1 hour, or overnight.

❋ Using only 4 or 5 pieces per skewer, skewer meat. Using real charcoal, grill meat until completely cooked, but still tender.

Babi Kecap
PORK IN KECAP SAUCE

Chef's Notes:
*When cutting and trimming your meat, reserve
some of the fat to use as grease for your wok,
rather than oil. Using the fat from the meat,
helps to maintain a consistent taste. Whereas,
using different oils can impart different flavors
to the dish. Best when served with rice, Krupuk*

Dish #4

1 1/2 lbs	Pork (any cut)
	Salt, to taste
	Pepper, to taste
	Juice of half a lemon
	Dash of sugar
2-3 tbsp	Kecap
1	Red chilie, minced and unseeded
5-6	Scallions, minced
3	Cloves garlic, minced
2 tsp	Ginger (jahe) (minced or powdered)
1/2 cup	Hot water

❀ Cut meat into 1-inch cubes, reserving fat*. Set aside. In bowl, combine salt, pepper, lemon juice, sugar and kecap. Add red chilies, scallions, garlic and ginger. Add meat, tossing to coat, and marinate in refrigerator for at least 1 hour, or over night.

❀ Heat wok, using some of the reserved fat to grease surface. Add meat and water, reduce heat to low and let simmer until all fluid has evaporated and meat is completely cooked. (If water evaporates before meat is done, add 2 tbsp of water at a time, until meat is cooked.

*See Chef's Notes

Sayur Currie Java
CURRIED JAVA SOUP

Chef's Notes:
This soup tastes wonderful when served with white rice, Goreng Timpi, (sautéed soy bean cakes), Lapjes Ayam (boned chicken fried in an egg batter), and a cucumber salad.

Dish #5

1 lb	Beef poulet, (stew meat) cut into bite-sized pieces
4 cups	Water
4	Scallions, finely minced
2	Cloves garlic, finely minced
1	Red chilie, finely minced (or 1 tbsp of any dried red pepper)
1 tbsp	Ginger (jahe)
1 tsp	Turmeric (kunyit)
1 tbsp	Coriander (ketumbar)
1/2 tsp	Cumin (jintan)
1 tsp	Shrimp paste (trassi)
2 tbsp	Butter
1	Lemon grass blade (sereh)
1	Large Bay leaf (daun salam)
1 cup	Green beans, diced
5	Potatoes, peeled and cut into bite-sized pieces
8 oz	Coconut milk
3	Bouillon cubes (beef or chicken flavor)
1/2 tsp	Sugar

❋ To create the beef stock, simmer meat in water for 1 hour. Meanwhile, in wok set on medium heat, sauté the scallions, garlic, red chilies, ginger, turmeric, coriander, cumin and shrimp paste in butter for 3-4 minutes. Add the lemon grass and bay leaf and let simmer 2 minutes. Remove from heat, adding it to the beef stock and let simmer in the beef stock for a few minutes. Add the green beans and potatoes. Cover and simmer a few more minutes. Add the coconut milk, bouillon cubes and sugar. Simmer, uncovered, for 2-3 minutes or until vegetables are cooked.

Serundeng I
SPICED SHREDDED COCONUT WITH PEANUTS

Chef's Notes:
Serundeng can be served with plain white rice and a sayur as a side dish. It can also be stored for a long period of time in the refrigerator.

Dish #6

1 tsp	Coriander (ketumbar)
1/2 tsp	Cumin (jinten)
4 tbsp	Fresh, minced onion
1 tsp	Fresh, minced garlic
	Salt, to taste
1 tsp	Java sugar (gula jawa)
2 tbsp	Oil
1 tsp	Tamarind (asam) mixed w/enough water to form a paste (or can use tamarind jelly)
1 tbsp	Lemon juice
3 tbsp	Coconut milk
2 cups	Shredded coconut
1 cup	Any good-quality roasted peanuts

❈ Heat oil in wok. Combine coriander, cumin, onion, garlic, salt and java sugar and sauté for 2 minutes over medium heat Add tamarind paste (or jelly), lemon juice, coconut milk and shredded coconut. Simmer on low until coconut is light brown and dry. Season with salt, if desired. Let cool. Add the peanuts, stir and serve or store in a glass container in refrigerator.

Ikan Bumbu Bali
FISH IN A HOT PAPRIKA SAUCE

Chef's Notes:
Serve this dish with white rice, cooked summer vegetables and cucumbers, (Atjar Kitimun).

Dish #7

1 lb	Cod, mackerel or haddock
3	Cloves garlic, minced
4	Scallions, minced
4	Red chilies, minced (or 2-3 paprikas, minced)
2 tbsp	Butter
1 tsp	Salt
1 tsp	Sugar
1 tsp	Laos powder or 2 inches fresh
2	Small bay leaves (daun salam)
1/2 tsp	Shrimp paste (trassi)
1 cup	Hot water
2 tbsp	Vinegar
11/2 tbsp	Kecap
1	Lemon grass blade

❀ To prepare, completely fry or bake the fish. Set aside. In wok, set on medium heat, sauté the garlic, scallions and chilies (or paprikas) in butter for a few minutes. Add the salt, sugar, laos, bay leaves and shrimp paste. Stir. Add the hot water, vinegar, kecap and lemon grass and let simmer for 8-10 minutes. Add the fish, in one whole piece, and continue simmering, covered, for 8 minutes.

RICE

Dish #8

❀ Rice is a mainstay of the Indonesian's diet. It is served with mostly every meal. There are two ways in which rice can be prepared - on the stove top using a pot or in a rice steamer or kukusan.

❀ If preparing rice on the stove top, be sure to use a heavy stainless steel pan, that has a thick bottom and a lid. Whenever possible use American rice. It is the best in the world. As it is mechanically processed prior to packaging, you do not need to rinse American rice. However, if using imported rice, rinse thoroughly.

❀ Place desired amount of rice (generally 2 cups of uncooked rice will serve four people) in pan. Cover rice with one inch of cold water. Over medium heat, bring to a boil. Reduce heat to simmer and cover with lid. Continue simmering until water is completely absorbed and rice is tender but dry. Remove from heat and fluff with fork. Keep pan covered with lid until ready to serve, so that heat and moisture stay in and rice does not become too dry.

❀ To prepare rice using a rice steamer (kukusan), place rice in top part of steamer. Cover rice with one inch of cold water and salt (or can use chicken-flavored bouillon cube in place of salt). Bring to a boil. Reduce heat and simmer until water is absorbed. Fill the bottom part with one half to one inch of water. Insert top part and lid. Bring to a boil, reduce heat and let simmer until rice is dry but tender. Fluff with fork.

Acar Ketimun Biasa
ORDINARY CUCUMBER SALAD

1	Cucumber
1 tbsp	Salt
2 tbsp	Sugar
2-3 tbsp	White vinegar
2-3	Scallions, minced
2	Red chilies, unseeded and minced

Chef's Notes:
When serving this salad, use a slotted spoon.
It helps to drain off some of the fluid.

Dish #9

❋ Grate or finely slice cucumber, with skin on, and place in a glass bowl. Set aside. In a separate bowl, combine salt, sugar and vinegar. Stir. Pour mixture over cucumbers and stir again. Sprinkle cucumbers with scallions and red chilies. Stir, cover and store in refrigerator until ready to serve. Salad should be served cold.

Dadar Ati
OMELET WITH CHICKEN LIVERS

Chef's Notes:
Dadar Ati can be used as an appetizer or as a main dish when served with rice and a cucumber or beet salad.

Dish #10

4	Eggs
4 tbsp	Milk
1/4 tsp	Aromat (Maggi Dutch soy sauce)
1/4 tsp	Pepper
5 tbsp	Butter
2 cups	Chicken livers
1/2 cup	Water
1 1/2	Cloves garlic, minced
3	Sprigs Soup celery, finely minced
2 tsp	Chives
Pinch	Tarragon
Pinch	Thyme
Dash	Salt, to taste
1 tbsp	Flour
1 tbsp	Cooking sherry

✻ In small mixing bowl, combine eggs with milk, 1/4 tsp aromat and pepper. In skillet melt 2 tbsp of butter and make 4 omelets, set aside. In wok, set on medium heat, sauté the chicken livers in 3 tbsp of butter until half done. Remove the chicken livers, cut into small pieces and then return them to the wok. Add water, garlic, celery, chives, tarragon, thyme and salt. Simmer over medium heat, stirring constantly until done. In a cup, dissolve flour with 1/4 tsp soy sauce and cooking sherry and add to the mixture. Stir until sauce begins to thicken. Remove from heat.

✻ *To serve:* Place omelets on a warm platter. Fill the omelets with chicken-liver mixture and roll the omelets up.

SATAY
(SATE OR KABOBS)

Satay, similar to American kabobs, are a tasty treat. As they are with my family, they are sure to become one of you and your family's favorites. For any holiday or special event for which I am usually cooking Indonesian, the one dish that everyone searches out for, when they come through the door, is the Satay.

Tender morsels of meat are marinated, then skewered and grilled. Generally, they are served with a variety of sauces*, but are perfectly delicious when eaten plain.

Satay is a perfect dish to prepare for parties or special occasions and can be prepared ahead of time.

For all of the Satay recipes in this chapter, grilling, using real charcoal is preferable, as the end result in taste is far better. However, a gas grill can certainly be used.

See Sauces for Satay Sauces

Satay Babi, II
SKEWERED INDONESIAN PORK SATE

Chef's Notes:
This is a very simple recipe and tastes different from the other Satay Babi.

1 lb.	Pork
1/2 tsp	Laos
	Salt, to taste
1	8 ounce can coconut milk
1/2 cup	Oil
	Skewers (small wooden kind, usually sold 100 per bag)

Sauce:

3 tbsp	Kecap manis (sweet soy sauce)
1/2 Cup	Water
1 tbsp	Tamarind (asam), mixed w/enough water to form a thin paste (or can use tamarind jelly)
1/2 tsp	Shrimp paste (trassi)
1 tbsp	Red chilies, minced and crushed
1	Onion, minced or 2 scallions, minced

❋ Cut meat into bite-sized cubes and combine with curry, salt and coconut milk. Let marinate for at least 1 hour. In wok, brown marinated meat in oil until half done. Let meat cool, then skewer meat, 4-5 pieces per skewer. Using real charcoal, (can use gas grill, but real charcoal tastes better) grill meat until completely cooked, but still tender.

❋ *To prepare the sauce:* Simmer together; kecap, water, tamarind paste, shrimp paste, red chilies, and onion (or scallions) until onions are done.

❋ *To serve:* Place barbecued satay on serving dish and cover with the sauce, reserving some sauce to be served on the side.

Satay-Bumbu-Kuning
MARINATED BEEF SATE

Chef's Notes:
When serving, choose a refreshing Atjar with rice and one of the hot relishes from the Sambal chapter.

1 lb.	Beef (any cut of steak)
3	Scallions, minced
3	Cloves garlic, minced
1-2	Red chilies, unseeded and minced
2-3	Almonds, minced and crushed
1 tsp	Salt
1/2 tsp	Java Sugar (gula jawa)
1/4 tsp	Shrimp paste (trassi)
Dash	Coriander powder (ketumbar)
1 tsp	Kurkumaplant powder (kunir)
Dash	Laos
1/2 tsp	Tamarind (asam), mixed w/enough water to form a thin paste (or can use tamarind jelly)
2 tbsp	Butter
1 Cup	Hot water
8 oz	Coconut milk
	Skewers (small wooden kind, usually sold 100 per bag)

❀ Slice meat into 1-inch cubes, set aside. Combine scallions, garlic, red chilies, almonds and crush together. Add to this the salt, java sugar, shrimp paste, coriander, kurkumaplant, laos, and tamarind paste. Stir. Using a wok, sauté this mixture in butter until scallions are light brown. Add hot water and coconut milk. Simmer 2 minutes then remove from heat and let cool. Add meat cubes, cover and store in refrigerator for at least 1 hour or over night (tastes better).

❀ Using only 4-5 pieces of meat per skewer, skewer meat. Using real charcoal, (can use gas grill, but charcoal tastes better than gas grilling), cook meat until done.

Satay Ajam
LEMONY CHICKEN SATE

4	Chicken breasts
2	Cloves garlic, minced and crushed
1 tsp	Laos
	Salt, to taste
	Pepper to taste
2 tbsp	Butter
2 tbsp	Kecap manis (sweet soy sauce)
	Juice of 1 lemon
	Skewers (small wooden kind, usually sold 100 per bag)

Chef's Notes:
Any combination of sayurs will add to this meal. Use the Sambal Kecap, shown in this cookbook, as a delicious sauce.

❀ Cut meat into 1-inch cubes, set aside. In a ceramic or glass bowl, combine garlic and laos. Add salt and pepper, stir. In a separate pan, melt butter then remove from heat. To this add Kecap and lemon juice. Combine both mixtures in the ceramic bowl, mixing thoroughly. Add the meat cubes, stir. Cover and let marinate in refrigerator for at least 1 hour, or overnight.

❀ Using only 4 or 5 pieces per skewer, skewer meat. Using real charcoal, grill meat until completely cooked, but still tender.

Satay Pentol
GROUND PORK SATE-CROQUETS

Chef's Notes:
Traditionally, this recipe calls for croquets to be skewered. However, this can be tricky. Therefore baking or frying the croquets is fine. If baking, you can use skewers, placing the skewered croquets on a baking sheet. If frying, do not use skewers. Simply drop croquets into heated oil.

16 oz	Ground Pork
2	Small eggs, beaten
4 tbsp	Coconut, shredded
2	Red Chilies, unseeded and minced
2-3	Almond nuts, crushed
2	Cloves garlic, minced
1/2 tsp	Coriander seed (ketumbar), crushed
2	Scallions, minced
1/2 tsp	Tamarind (asam), mixed w/ enough water to form a paste (or can use tamarind jelly)
1/4 tsp	Cumin (jintan)
1/2 tsp	Shrimp paste (trassi)
1 tsp	Salt
1/2 tsp	Sugar
	Oil for frying (optional)
	Skewers (optional)

✽ In large bowl, combine meat with eggs and coconut. To this add peppers, almond nuts, garlic, coriander, scallions, tamarind, cumin and shrimp paste. Stir. Add salt and sugar, stir. Add all ingredients to meat mixture and combine completely.

✽ Using your hands, make croquet forms and skewer. (Or, if frying, only make croquet form.) Grill, bake or fry*.

*See chef's notes.

Satay Manis
SWEET BEEF SATE

Chef's Notes:
I suggest serving this with white rice and either Sayur Lodeh or Sayur Gudek. (Both are in the Sops and Sayurs chapter).

1 lb	Beef (any cut)
2-3	Cloves garlic, finely minced
2-3	Scallions, finely minced
1 tsp	Tamarind (asam), mixed with enough water to form a paste (or can use tamarind jelly)
1/2 tsp	Salt (or more, to taste)
2 tsp	Java sugar (gula-jawa)
1 tbsp	Butter
2 tbsp	Kecap manis (sweet soy sauce)
	Juice of 1 lemon
	Skewers (small wooden kind, usually sold 100 per bag)

❀ Cut meat into 1-inch cubes, set aside. In a ceramic or glass bowl, combine garlic, scallions and tamarind. To this add salt and java sugar. Stir. In a separate pan, melt butter, then remove from heat. To this, add kecap and lemon juice. Mix. Combine both mixtures in the ceramic or glass bowl, mixing thoroughly. Add the meat cubes, Stir. Cover and let marinate in refrigerator for at least 1 hour, or overnight.

❀ Using only 4 or 5 pieces per skewer, skewer meat. Using real charcoal, grill meat until completely cooked, but still tender

SatayAjam with a Peanut Butter Sauce
CHICKEN SATE WITH A SPICY PEANUT BUTTER SAUCE

Chef's Notes:
This is a simple dish to prepare and is delicious served with white rice.

1	Large Chicken, cut up
4 tbsp	Kecap
	Salt, to taste
	Pepper, to taste

Sauce:

8 tbsp	Water
4 tbsp	Peanut butter
1/2 tsp	Crushed red pepper
1/2 tsp	Maple Syrup
1 tbsp	Kecap

❋ Remove chicken from bone and cut chicken into 1-inch pieces. Marinate chicken in kecap, salt and pepper for at least 2 hours, or overnight. Once chicken is completely marinated, skewer meat, using 4-5 pieces per skewer. Using real charcoal, grill meat until completely cooked, but still tender.

❋ *To make the sauce:* use a medium-sized sauce pan and simmer together the water, peanut butter, red pepper, maple syrup and kecap. Let simmer, on low heat, until smooth. Pour sauce over barbecued chicken and serve.

MEAT DISHES

There are many types of meat available to the Indonesian. Beef, pork and lamb are the most common. Beef is very expensive and the taste is different than the U.S. beef. Indonesian beef has a gamy taste. I think that is one of the reasons that so many spices are used in its preparation. They are needed to help over come the gaminess that is associated with it. The Water Buffalo and the Humpback White Brahma Steer are the most common animals used for beef. They are also used for other tasks - primarily hauling carts and plowing the rice fields.

Pork is also a common source of food. My father, who liked to hunt in his spare time, was quite a hunter of big game. (Crocodile hunting was one of his big challenges). He was approached, many times, by the villagers who were seeking his assistance in ridding themselves of the wild boars These pesky beasts were destroying the protective walls that surrounded the rice fields. Boars produce an abundance of offspring and keeping their population down to an acceptable level was a big challenge.

I remember my father had brought home a baby pig who he put in a bamboo-fenced pen. The little pig grew amazingly fast and soon was a big, fat pig with enormous tusks. After a while he dug himself out of the pen and took a stroll through town. I think that was the first pig hunt that was done "in town" by my father. After a few "breakouts" and numerous complaints by the neighbors, my father had no choice but to shoot the animal. There was a large Chinese family that lived near us who were delighted to receive the animal. It fed their family for many, many days.

Frikadel Ketimun
STUFFED CUCUMBERS OVER CHINESE NOODLES

Chef's Notes:
This recipe calls for three slices of soaked bread. To do this, use day old white bread (or leave slices out for a few hours or overnight). Remove crust and tear bread into small pieces. Combine with two tbs. of milk and toss until all the bread pieces become moist.

4	Cucumbers
1 lb	Lean ground beef
3 slices	Soaked white bread*
1/2	Egg, beaten
1/2 tsp	Salt
1/4 tsp	Pepper
1/4 tsp	Lemon juice
1 cup	Water
1	Onion, minced
2 tbsp	Butter
1 tbsp	Kecap
1 lb	Chinese noodles (can use vermicelli as a substitute)

❋ Cut cucumbers in half, lengthwise and remove seeds. Hollow the inside out. Set aside. In mixing bowl, combine ground beef, soaked bread, eggs, salt, pepper and lemon juice. Using your hands, knead mixture thoroughly.

❋ Fill cucumbers with the meat filling and place in a buttered casserole dish. Add 1 cup of water. Top the cucumbers with some dots of butter. In wok, sauté onions with a little bit of oil for a few minutes. Add butter and kecap. Pour over casserole and place casserole dish in 350° preheated oven for 30-40 minutes, or until meat is fully cooked. Cook Chinese noodles according to package instructions.

❋ *To serve:* Place cooked noodles on large platter and cover with stuffed cucumbers.

* See Chef's Notes

Den Deng Ragi, II
DRIED STEAK WITH COCONUT AND PEANUTS

Chef's Notes:
This recipe is similar to Den Deng Ragi, I, but is a bit more flavorful, due to the additional spices that are used. The peanuts also add a pleasant texture. This dish can also be stored in the refrigerator for long periods of time.

1 lb	Steak, any cut
2 tbsp	Kecap
1/2 tsp	Salt
1 tbsp	Oil or butter
2	Cloves garlic, minced
5	Scallions, minced
1 tsp	Coriander seed (ketumbar)
1/2 tsp	Laos, fresh or powdered
1 1/2 tsp	Java Sugar (gula jawa)
1/2 tsp	Shrimp paste (trassi)
8 oz	Coconut, shredded
2	Small Bay leaves (daun salam)
1 tsp	Tamarind (asam) mixed w/ enough water to form a paste (or can use tamarind jelly)
4 oz	Roasted Peanuts

✱ Cut meat into long thin strips (about 1/4 inch wide by 3-4 inches long). Rub meat with kecap and 1 part of the salt (about 1/4 tsp). Using a wok set on medium heat, sauté meat in oil or butter until fully cooked. Remove meat from wok and set aside. In small bowl crush together: garlic, coriander seed, laos, java sugar, shrimp paste and remainder of salt. Add coconut, bay leaf and tamarind paste. Stir. Heat oil in wok, then reduce heat to simmer. Combine all ingredients in wok, except peanuts, and let simmer until coconut is a light-brown color. (Stir constantly being careful that coconut does not darken too quickly). Remove from heat and stir in peanuts. Let cool completely before serving.

Frikadel Kool
STUFFED CABBAGE·LEAVES

Chef's Notes:
To cook cabbage leaves you can either sauté in a wok or bake in a casserole dish in the oven. I find it easiest to bake in the oven

1 lb	Lean ground beef (80-90% lean)
1/2 tsp	Salt
1/4 tsp	Pepper
Dash	Nutmeg
1 1/2 tbsp	Kecap
1/2 tsp	Ginger powder (jahe)
3	Eggs, beaten
1-2 tbsp	Mashed potatoes
2 tbsp	Milk
8-10	Cabbage leaves
	Hot Water
1	Stick of butter
	Toothpicks

❋ In large bowl, combine meat with salt, pepper, nutmeg, kecap, ginger and eggs. Add potatoes and milk and mix thoroughly. Blanch cabbage leaves in boiling water for a few seconds. Drain and fill cabbage leaves with meat mixture. Wrap cabbage leaves and secure with a toothpick. Sauté stuffed cabbage leaves in wok with 1 stick of melted butter or bake in oven at 350° for 30-40 minutes, or until done.

Empal Daging II
MONKEY HAIR II
(SAUTÉED SIRLOIN STEAK)

Chef's Notes:
This recipe is affectionately titled Monkey Hair because of the appearance of the meat when it is fully cooked. The meat is first simmered in coconut milk and spices, cooled and then cooked again until it becomes dry and shredded.

12 oz	Sirloin steak
8 oz	Coconut milk
2 tbsp	Tamarind mixed w/enough water to form a paste (or can use tamarind jelly)
	Salt, to taste
1/2 tsp	Coriander seed (ketumbar)
1/2 tsp	Laos
16 oz	Water
2 tbsp	Butter or Oil

❀ Cut meat into 1/2 inch by 4-inch strips cutting with the grain of the meat. In wok set on medium heat, simmer meat in coconut milk, uncovered, for 5 minutes. Add tamarind, salt, coriander seed and laos. Continue simmering until all the fluid is gone. Remove from heat and let cool completely. Return meat to wok and brown meat in a little bit of butter or oil until meat is almost completely dry and crispy.

Rempah
MEATBALLS IN A COCONUT SAUCE

Chef's Notes:
Rempah makes a nice combination when served with Nassi Gurih (Fragrant Rice). They can also be used as a side dish in your Reistaffel.

2	Lemon leaves (jeruk purut)
1	Screw pine leaf (daun pan dan)
8 oz	Hot water
1 tsp	Tamarind (asam) mixed w/enough water to form a paste (or can use tamarind jelly)
1/4 cup	Coconut milk (or more)
1 tsp	Lemon grass powder (sereh)
1/2 tsp	Salt (or more, to taste)
1 lb	Lean ground beef (80-90% lean)
2	Eggs, beaten
1/4 tsp	Pepper
3 tbsp	Butter or oil

❀ Soak lemon leaves and pan dan leaves in 8 ounces of hot water for 5 minutes. Drain and set aside. In wok, sauté in butter the tamarind, coconut milk, lemon grass powder, salt, lemon leaves and pan dan leaves for 10 minutes. Remove from heat and set aside. In bowl, combine ground beef, eggs, pepper and the sautéed mixture, mix thoroughly. (If mixture seems a bit dry, add additional coconut milk). Make small meat balls, about 1 inch in diameter. Brown meatballs in butter or oil until completely cooked.

Semoor Lapies
STEAK STRIPS IN BREAD CRUMBS

Chef's Notes:
Serve with white rice, various vegetables,
sambals, relishes, krupuk and a desert of fruit
and jello pudding or fruit with vanilla sauce for
a delightful summer treat.

3/4-1 lb	Steak, any cut
	Salt, to taste
	Pepper, to taste
Dash	Nutmeg
1	Egg, beaten
	Bread crumbs (plain)
4	Small onions, cut into large pieces
3 tbsp	Butter or oil
2 cups	Hot water
3 tbsp	Kecap manis

❋ Cut steak into evenly-sized thin strips. Rub meat with salt, pepper and nutmeg. Set aside. In large glass bowl, beat egg. Add meat and stir. Add bread crumbs, stir again and set aside. In wok, set on medium heat, sauté onions in butter or oil until light brown. Add meat and brown meat on both sides. Add hot water and simmer for 2 minutes. Add kecap, stir and cover pan. Let simmer until meat is tender, but cooked, (at least 2 hours). Check water level often, adding more hot water as necessary so that meat is served in a sauce.

Bumbu Bali Beef
MARINATED BEEF

12 oz	Beef, any cut
3	Red chilies, unseeded and minced
3-4	Scallions, minced
1	Clove garlic, minced
1/2 tsp	Tamarind (asam), mixed w/enough water to form a paste (or can use tamarind jelly)
1/4 tsp	Shrimp paste (trassi)
1 inch	Laos, grated or 1 tsp powder
2	Bay leaves (daun salam)
1	Lemon grass blade (sereh)
2 tbsp	Butter
2 tbsp	Kecap
1 tbsp	Java Sugar (gula jawa)
1	Beef bouillon cube
8 oz	Hot water

Chef's Notes:
Serve the Marinated Beef with white rice, krupuk, and sambals (hot chili relish) as well as one of your favorite sayurs (soups).

❀ Cut meat into 1/2 inch by 3 inch strips, set aside. Crush together: red chilies, scallions, garlic, tamarind, shrimp paste, laos and bay leaves. Sauté the lemon grass twig (left in one piece and removed after dish is completely cooked) and all of the crushed ingredients in butter for 5 minutes. Add meat, kecap, java sugar, bouillon cube and hot water. Cover and let simmer until meat is done, stirring occasionally. Check water level often, adding more hot water as necessary, so that meat is served in a sauce.

Frikadel Goreng
BAKED MEATBALLS

Chef's Notes:
This recipe is the Indonesian interpretation of Swedish meatballs, except that they are generally baked in an oven, rather than fried. However, if frying is preferred, they will still be tasty. They can be used as a side dish or appetizer.

2	Eggs, beaten
12 oz	Lean ground beef (80-90% lean)
3 tbsp	Mashed potatoes
1	Clove garlic, minced and crushed
2	Scallions, finely minced
Dash	Nutmeg
Dash	Cloves, freshly ground or powder
	Pepper, to taste
1	Bouillon cube, dissolved in 2 tbsp of hot water
	Butter or oil (*if frying)

❀ In large bowl, combine eggs with meat, mashed potatoes, garlic, scallions, nutmeg, cloves and pepper. Dissolve the bouillon cube in 2 tbsp of hot water and add to mixture. Mix thoroughly. Using your hands, make meatballs, about 1 inch in diameter. Place meatballs on ungreased cookie sheet and bake in preheated 350° oven until meatballs are brown and completely cooked.

❀ If frying, be sure to use butter or oil and cook on medium heat until brown and completely cooked.

*See Chef's Notes

Rempah Meatballs
SMALL MEATBALLS

Chef's Notes:
These small but tasty meatballs make for a quick and easy appetizer or the perfect side dish. They can be made a day in advance and reheat well.
For additional taste, meatballs cam be rolled in egg whites and bread crumbs and baked until brown and done.

1 lb	Lean ground beef (80-90% lean)
1 tbsp	Minced red chilies (or Sambal Ulek)
1/2 tsp	Coriander seed (ketumbar)
Dash	Laos
Dash	Ground cloves
1/2 tsp	Freshly minced garlic, crushed
1/2 tsp	Onion powder
1 tbsp	Corn starch
	Salt, to taste
1	Egg yolk (reserving the egg white)*
8 oz	Shredded coconut
	Oil or butter (if frying)
	Bread crumbs (optional)

✸ In large bowl, combine meat with all of the ingredients, except the coconut. Mix thoroughly by kneading with your hands. Once mixture is completely mixed, add the coconut and knead again. Using your hands, make small meatballs (about 1 inch in diameter) and place them on an ungreased cookie sheet and bake in 350° oven for 20-30 minutes, or until fully cooked. If frying, heat butter or oil on medium heat and cook meatballs until fully cooked. Serve Hot.

*See Chef's Notes

Digoreng Paprika
INDONESIAN STUFFED PEPPERS

Chef's Notes:
This dish is very similar to the traditional "American" stuffed peppers, but with an Indonesian twist.

2	Green peppers
2	Red peppers
1 lb	Lean ground beef (80-90% lean)
2	Eggs, beaten
1	Clove garlic, minced
1	Large Onion, minced
1/2 tsp	Salt
1/4 tsp	Pepper
Dash	Nutmeg
Dash	Sugar
2 tbsp	Mashed potatoes
1 tbsp	Kecap manis
2 tbsp	Butter

❋ Prepare peppers by cutting them in half and removing seeds. Rinse peppers and set aside. Combine ground beef with eggs, garlic, onion, salt, pepper, nutmeg, sugar, potatoes and kecap. Mix thoroughly. Fill peppers with ground beef mixture. Place stuffed peppers into a buttered casserole dish. Cover and cook in 350° preheated oven for 30-45 minutes, or until meat is completely cooked. Serve hot.

❋ This can also be prepared on the stove top by cooking in a buttered casserole dish with the lid on. Use medium heat until mixture comes to a boil. Reduce heat to simmer and keep covered until meat is done. (Approximately 1 hour).

CHICKEN DISHES

The people who live in the small villages of Indonesia are generally poor. There is little or no refrigeration avialable to them. Therefore, a trip to the market is a part of their daily routine. This trip is ually quite a long one and haggling between buyer and seller is commonplace. Once an amicable deal is reached, they return to the village with the live chicken(s). The chickens are then beheaded and readied for that day's meals.

Because of the lack of refrigeration, the Indonesians have mastered the art of using every part of the chicken. If the chicken is removed from the bone, then the bones and carcass are used for soup. Necessity is the mother of invention, and the Indonesian people have certainly mastered it tastefully.

Pastel Tutup
CHICKEN AND CHAMPIGNON CASSEROLE

Chef's Notes:
This is a hearty and flavor-filled casserole that will quench the most veracious of appetites. Though there are many ingredients, it is a simple recipe. All of the vegetables and even the chicken can be cleaned and prepped a day in advance, making this casserole an impressive yet simple meal to prepare. Champignons (mushrooms) can be bought in most Indonesian and Chinese import stores and in some large grocery and health food stores.

1	Large chicken
	Water
1 cup	Lilly-white night champignons, cleaned
1 cup	Dried Chinese champignons, cleaned
2	Chicken-flavored bouillon cubes
1/2 head	Chinese cabbage, torn into large pieces
1/2 can	Peas
1 cup	Snow peas, cleaned, stems removed
2 cups	Boiled carrots (or 1 can whole)
2	Small leeks, sliced
4	Scallions, sliced
1/2	stick Butter
1 1/2 tbsp	Kecap
1/2 tsp	Pepper
1/2 tsp	Sugar
3	Hard boiled eggs, sliced in half
8	Potatoes, boiled & mashed with milk (or can use packaged potato puree)
1/3 cup	Bread crumbs (or more)

✳ In large pot, boil chicken in water until completely cooked. Remove chicken from pot, reserving broth. Remove meat from bone and cut into small pieces (about 2-3 inches wide). Set aside. Place champignons in a separate pot and cover with cold water. Bring to a boil, reduce heat and let simmer for 35 minutes, making sure champignons are covered with water at all times. Drain and set aside. Return the reserved bouillon to a boil. Add the chicken, champignons, bouillon cubes, cabbage, peas, snow peas and carrots. Let simmer 2-3 minutes. In wok, set on medium heat, sauté leek and scallions in 2 tbsp of butter for 3 minutes. To this, add the vegetables, kecap, pepper and sugar. Let simmer until cabbage is tender-crisp. Butter the inside of a casserole dish with 1 tbsp of butter. Place the chicken, champignons and vegetables in the casserole dish, spreading evenly. Next, make one layer with the sliced eggs, on top of this add the potato puree and then the bread crumbs. Lastly, drop small dots of butter over the top. Bake in a 350° oven for 30 minutes or until a golden brown on top

Ajam Bumbu Rujak
HOT SPICED CHICKEN

Chef's Notes:
Traditionally, this dish is served without a sauce. However, I prefer to serve it in a sauce, so that the chicken does not become too dry.

1	Chicken, cut into 4-inch pieces
1 tsp	Tamarind, mixed w/enough water to form a paste (or can use tamarind jelly)
	Salt, to taste
	Pepper, to taste
3 tbsp	Butter
5	Red chilies, unseeded and minced
2-3	Cloves garlic, minced
5-6	Scallions, minced
1/2 tsp	Shrimp paste (trassi)
4	Lemon leaves (jerukpurut)
2	Small bay leaves (daun salam)
1	Lemon grass blade, (sereh)
1/4 tsp	Laos
1	Chicken flavored bouillon cube
1 cup	Hot water
1 tsp	Java sugar (gula jawa)

❀ Cut chicken into small pieces and rub the chicken pieces on all sides with tamarind, salt and pepper. In wok, set on medium heat, sauté chicken in 2 tbsp of butter until done. In separate pan, using 1 tbsp of butter, sauté the red chilies, garlic, scallions and shrimp paste over medium heat for 3-4 minutes. Add the lemon leaves, bay leaves, lemon grass and laos. Stir. Combine all of the ingredients and place in the wok with the chicken. Add the hot water, bouillon cubes and java sugar and let simmer 10-15 minutes.

Opor Ajam
MILD SWEET CHICKEN IN A GINGER-COCONUT SAUCE

Chef's Notes:
Preparing this dish and letting it marinate overnight, will improve the flavor. Serve with Sambal Goreng Boontjes (Hot Sautéed Green Beans), krupuk and cucumber salad.

1	Whole chicken
3	Cloves garlic, minced
4	Scallions, minced
4	Almond nuts, minced and crushed
1/2 tsp	Shrimp paste (trassi)
	Water
1/2 tsp	Java Sugar (gula jawa)
1 tsp	Coriander seed (ketumbar)
4	Lemon leaves (jerukpurut)
1/2 tsp	Tamarind (asam) mixed w/enough water to make a paste (or can use tamarind jelly)
2-3	Bay leaves (daun salam)
1/2 tsp	Laos
1	Lemon grass blade
2	Chicken-flavored bouillon cubes
8 oz	Coconut milk

✺ Cut up chicken into small pieces, measuring about 3 inches. Set aside. Combine garlic, scallions, almond nuts and shrimp paste and use this combination to rub the chicken with on all sides. Place chicken in a large pan and cover with water. Bring to a boil, reduce heat. Add java sugar, coriander seed, lemon leaves, tamarind, bay leaves, laos and lemon grass. Continue simmering for 15 minutes. Add bouillon cubes and coconut milk. Stir and let simmer, uncovered, for 3 minutes or until chicken is completely cooked. Be sure to check the fluid level often, adding additional hot water as necessary.

Chicken Dishes

Ajam Ketjap
GRANDMA'S CHICKEN IN A KECAP SAUCE

Chef's Notes:
This was my grandmother's version of a popular Indonesian dish.

1	Whole chicken, cut up into small pieces
2 Cups	Water
1	Clove garlic, minced
	Salt, to taste
	Pepper, to taste
2 tbsp	Kecap (Indonesian soy sauce)
1/2 tsp	Sugar
2 tbsp	Bread crumbs (plain)
1	Chicken-flavored bouillon cube
2 tbsp	Butter

✹ In covered wok, boil chicken pieces in 2 cups of salted water until half done. Remove from heat. Remove chicken from wok and let cool, reserving the fluid left in wok. Set aside. Crush together the garlic, salt, pepper and kecap and rub chicken pieces with this mixture. Return chicken to wok, add sugar and simmer until almost done. Add bread crumbs, bouillon cube and butter. Continue simmering until chicken is completely cooked and no liquid remains.

Ajam Besengeh of Ajam Kuning

YELLOW CHICKEN IN A COCONUT SAUCE

Chef's Notes:
Combining this dish together with white rice, sate, and your choice of Sambal Goreng dishes, makes it a simple, but delicious meal.

1	Chicken, cut up
3-4	Cloves garlic, minced
2-3	Red chilies, minced
4	Scallions, minced
3-4	Almond nuts, minced and crushed
1/2 tsp	Shrimp paste (trassi)
3 tbs	Butter
1/2 tsp	Tamarind (asam) mixed w/enough water to form a paste (or can use tamarind jelly)
2 tsp	Ginger powder or 1 inch ginger root
1 tsp	Kurkumaplant (kunyit)
1/2 tsp	Coriander seed (ketumbar)
1	Lemon grass blade, (sereh)
2	Chicken flavored bouillon cubes
3 cups	Hot water
8 oz	Coconut milk
1/2 tsp	Java sugar (gula jawa)

❁ Cut up 1 whole chicken, set aside. In wok, set on medium heat, sauté the garlic, red chilies, scallions, almond nuts and shrimp paste in butter for 3-4 minutes. Add the tamarind, ginger, kurkumaplant, coriander seed and lemon grass and let simmer for 3-4 minutes. Add the chicken, bouillon cubes and water and continue simmering until chicken is done. Add coconut milk and sugar and simmer, uncovered for 10-15 minutes, stirring often.

Ajam Jintan
CHICKEN CUMIN IN A SAUCE

Chef's Notes:
As the salt content of bouillon cubes can vary greatly from one brand to the next, do not add salt until all of the ingredients have simmered together for a while. Be sure to taste-test before you add salt.

1	Whole chicken
2	Chicken-flavored bouillon cubes
1	Lemon grass blade, (sereh)
8 oz	Coconut milk
1	Red chilie, unseeded and minced
2	Small cloves garlic, minced
4	Scallions, minced
1 tsp	Cumin (jintan)
1 1/2 tsp	Coriander seed (ketumbar)
1/4 tsp	Laos
1 1/2 tsp	Kurkumaplant (kunyit)
Dash	Sugar

❋ Cut chicken into 2-3 inch pieces. Place chicken into large pot with enough cold water to completely cover chicken. Add bouillon cubes and bring water to a boil. Let boil for a few minutes. Reduce heat and add the lemon grass, coconut milk, red chilie, garlic, scallions, cumin, coriander seed, laos, kurkumaplant and sugar. Let simmer, uncovered, until chicken is completely done. Check water level often, adding additional hot water as necessary so that chicken is served in a sauce.

Kerrie Rebung Ajam
SPICED CHICKEN IN A BAMBOO SPROUT SAUCE

Chef's Notes:
This dish can be prepared a day in advance.
Serve with white rice and/or sate and a salad.

1	Whole chicken
	Water
1 can	Bamboo sprouts
2-3	Red chilies, minced
3-4	Scallions, minced
3	Cloves garlic, minced
1/2 tsp	Coriander seed (ketumbar)
1 tsp	Kurkumaplant plant (kunyit)
1/2 tsp	Tamarind mixed w/enough water to form a paste (or can use tamarind jelly)
1 tsp	Shrimp paste (trassi)
2 tbsp	Butter
Dash	Sugar
1-2	Chicken-flavored bouillon cubes
2	Small bay leaves
2 8 oz.	Cans Coconut milk

❋ Cut chicken into small pieces (about 2-3 inches square) and place in wok. Completely cover chicken with cold water and bring to a boil. Reduce heat and let simmer until chicken is done. In separate pan, boil bamboo sprouts for 8-10 minutes, or until tender. Remove bamboo sprouts, slice lengthwise and set aside. In small bowl, combine red chilies, scallions and garlic. Add coriander seed, kurkumaplant and shrimp paste. In wok, set on medium heat, melt butter. Add the spice combination and sauté for a few minutes. Add the chicken, cover and let simmer for 8-10 minutes. Add sugar, tamarind and bouillon cubes. Stir. Add bamboo sprouts and coconut milk and let simmer, uncovered, for 15-20 minutes. Check water level often, adding additional hot water as necessary so that chicken is served in a sauce

Ajam Pang Gang
BARBECUED CHICKEN

Chef's Notes:
I find it easiest to marinate the chicken using plastic zip-lock bags. Serve this dish with Urap, (vegetables with shredded coconut), cucumber salad, krupuk and sambals.

4 tbsp	Onion (or scallions if preferred)
3 tbsp	Maggi Dutch soy sauce
1/4 tsp	Pepper
1 tbsp	Butter, melted
1	Young chicken
	Lemon juice (optional)

❀ Mince and crush together the onion, Maggi Dutch soy sauce, pepper and melted butter. Set aside. Cut chicken in half at the breast bone (or, as an option, cut into large pieces). Rub chicken inside and out with the butter-spice mixture, being sure to completely cover the entire chicken with the marinade. Let marinate for at least 2 hours, (or preferably overnight), turning pieces occasionally, to coat. Once the chicken is completely marinated barbecue or broil the chicken until completely cooked. For an optional garnish, spritz the chicken with lemon juice just before serving.

Ajam Zwartzuur
CHICKEN IN A RED WINE SAUCE

Chef's Notes:
My grandmother served this dish with boiled potatoes instead of rice (as the traditional recipe does), with Boiled Pears as a side dish.

1	Chicken
	Salt, to taste
	Pepper, to taste
2 tbsp	Butter
3-4	Scallions, minced
1 1/2	Cups Red wine
2 tbsp	Sugar
6-7	Whole cloves
1	Cinnamon stick
Dash	Nutmeg
2 1/2 tbsp	Vinegar
1/2 - 1	Chicken-flavored bouillon cube

Boiled Pears:

2	Large cans of pears with juice, halved (can substitute with peaches)
1 tbsp	Vinegar
1 tsp	Whole cloves
1	Cinnamon stick

❋ Cut chicken into 2-inch by 3-inch pieces. Rub chicken on all sides with salt and pepper. In wok, sauté chicken in butter until light brown. Add scallions, wine, sugar, cloves, cinnamon stick, nutmeg and vinegar. Cover and let simmer 1 hour. Add bouillon cube and continue simmering until bouillon cube is completely dissolved. Be sure to check water level often, adding additional hot water as necessary so that meat is completely covered and to ensure enough sauce when serving.

❋ *To prepare the boiled pears:* Place pears, with their juices, in a medium sized pan and let simmer until juices begin to boil. Add vinegar, cloves and cinnamon stick and continue simmering for exactly 5 minutes. Remove from heat. Take out cloves and cinnamon stick and discard. Let pears cool completely.

Chicken Dishes

Ajam Semoor Jawa
JAVA-BOILED CHICKEN IN INDONESIAN SOY SAUCE

Chef's Notes:

For people who like rice served with a lot of fluid, this is the dish for them. Pour over white rice, served in a deep plate. It can be made a day in advance and is easy to prepare. Serve with krupuk and a refreshing salad.

1	Whole chicken
	Juice of 1 lemon
3 tbsp	Kecap
2 tbsp	Butter
2 cups	Hot water
3	Chicken-flavored bouillon cubes
3	Whole cloves
2	Cloves garlic, minced
2-3	Whole red chilies, seeds removed
3-4	Onions, cut into large pieces
Dash	Sugar

✤ Cut up chicken into large pieces. Rub the chicken on all sides with lemon juice and kecap. Using a wok, set on high heat, melt butter. Add chicken and brown on both sides. Add hot water and bouillon cubes. Cover and let simmer for 15-20 minutes. Add cloves, garlic, red chilies, onions and sugar. Cover and let simmer 15 minutes. Check fluid level often, adding additional hot water as necessary so that chicken is served in a plentiful sauce.

Ajam Rendang
SPICY COCONUT CHICKEN

Chef's Notes:
This is a quick and easy recipe that is full of flavor. If preferred, you can create a smaller version of this dish by using only half a chicken and reducing the ingredients by half.

6	Red chilies, unseeded and crushed
1	Finger length of Turmeric, grated (kunyit)
	Salt, to taste
1 tbsp	Cold water
1	Chicken, cut into small pieces
16 oz	Coconut milk

❀ Crush together the chilies, turmeric and salt with 1 tbsp cold water. Using a wok, set on medium heat, sauté the crushed ingredients, chicken and coconut milk, for a few minutes. Stir, reduce heat and let simmer, uncovered, until no fluid remains, stirring occasionally.

Pedas Ajam Rendang
SPICY CUBED CHICKEN IN A COCONUT BATH

Chef's Notes:
This is the dish for those who like hot spicy food. Serve with a sayur, white rice, salads and lots of fruit to cool your pallet.

1	Whole chicken
8	Red chilies, minced
1/2 tsp	Shrimp paste (trassi)
6-7	Red onions, minced
2-3	White onions, minced
1 tsp	Laos
8 oz	Shredded coconut
2 tbsp	Butter
8 oz	Coconut milk
2	Bay leaves (daun salam)
1	Lemon grass blade (sereh)
1 tbsp	Lemon juice

❉ Cut chicken into 3-4 inch pieces. Set aside. Combine chilies, shrimp paste, red onions, white onions, laos and coconut and using wok, sauté in butter until onions are half cooked. Add chicken, coconut milk, bay leaves and lemon grass. Continue simmering until chicken is done and all fluid has evaporated. If desired, sprinkle dish with lemon juice prior to serving.

FISH

Fish and rice is the main dish of the villagers of Indonesia and it is prepared in a variety of different ways - boiled, grilled, dried, etc.

Indonesia is made up of over 13,000 islands. Each seaside village boasts a fish market. Small amounts of fish are strung on bamboo poles and carried through the streets to the nearest villages to sell. Larger amounts are carried by motorized vehicles - sometimes a small pick up truck or by tricycles, loaded with baskets full of different kinds of fish. The housewife will usually send her Koki (chef) to the market, where everything is purchased for that days' dinner.

There are many different kinds of fish available to the housewife or chef in Indonesia. Many of the common types are not available in the United States, but the American fish markets supply us with enough variety to use as a substitution.

Rempejek Udang
SHRIMP RICE FLOUR COOKIES

2 cups	Rice flour
2-3	Cloves garlic, finely minced
1	Red chilie, unseeded and finely minced
1	Scallion, finely minced
1/4 tsp	Pepper
1/4 tsp	Cumin (jintan)
1/2 tsp	Coriander (ketumbar)
*4 oz	Coconut milk
1/2 tsp	Tamarind (asam)
1 tsp	Salt
1/2 lb	Small cooked shrimp
	Oil

Chef's Notes:
When adding the coconut milk to the batter, start with only 2 ounces. Then increase accordingly so that the batter attains a thick, paste-like consistency. If batter becomes too thin, add some additional flour or if too thick, add water, a few drops at a time.

Serving white rice and any kind of sayur will compliment these cookies nicely.

❀ In large mixing bowl, combine flour with garlic, red chili, scallion, pepper, cumin and coriander. Add coconut milk*, tamarind and salt. Mix thoroughly, making a thick paste. Add shrimp and stir. In wok, set on high, heat oil. Using two spoons, scoop up mixture and drop into hot oil. Let simmer until a golden brown.

***See Chef's notes.**

Ikan Lombok (Jeruk & Tomat)
SPICY LEMON AND TOMATO FISH

Chef's Notes:
This recipe is perfect for the person who is short on time, but still wants to make a delicious meal. The fish can be broiled ahead of time and then quickly prepared for that days meal.

2 tbsp	Butter
2-3	Scallions, minced
2	Small red chilies, minced
2-3	Red tomatoes, sliced
1 tsp	Salt
1 Cup	Hot water
	Juice of 1 lemon
1 1/2 lb	Broiled cod or haddock
2 tbsp	Chives
1/2 tsp	Ginger (jahe)
Dash	Sugar

✳ In wok, set on medium heat, sauté in butter the scallions and hot peppers for 2-3 minutes. Add the tomato slices, salt, hot water and lemon juice and let simmer for 3 minutes. Add the broiled fish, chives, ginger and sugar. Cover and let simmer 7 minutes.

Pindang Ikan
FISH COOKED SLOWLY IN SPICES

Chef's Notes:
Serve this dish with white rice.

1 1/2 lb	Cod or haddock, uncooked
	Juice of 1 lemon
3-4	Scallions, minced
3	Cloves garlic, minced
2	Red chilies, minced
2 tbsp	Butter
2 inches	Laos or 1 1/2 tsp powder
1/2 tsp	Shrimp paste (trassi)
1 tsp	Kurkumaplant powder(kunyit)
2 cups	Hot water
2	Indonesian bay leaves (daun salam)
1	Lemon grass blade
1 1/2 tsp	Tamarind (asam) mixed w/enough water to form a paste (or can use tamarind jelly)
1 tsp	Salt
1/2 lb	Chinese cabbage, shredded
Dash	Sugar

❋ Clean fish and rub with lemon juice. Set aside for 15 minutes. Using wok, set on medium heat, sauté the scallions, garlic and red chilies in butter for 2-3 minutes. Add the laos, shrimp paste and kurkumaplant. Stir and let simmer 1 minute. Add water and fish and simmer 5 minutes. Add the bay leaves, lemon grass, tamarind and salt. Cover and let simmer for 1/2 hour. Add cabbage and sugar and continue simmering until cabbage is cooked but crisp.

Fish Dishes

Kerrie Ikan
CURRIED FISH

Chef's Notes:
Serve with white rice, cucumber salad and krupuk. I also like to serve either fruit salads or a variety of fruits placed on a large, round platter.

1 1/2 lb	Cod or haddock, uncooked
	Salt, to taste
1 tbsp	Tamarind (asam)
	Water
2 tbsp	Butter
1	Clove garlic, minced
1	Red chilie, unseeded and minced
4	Scallions, minced
1/4 tsp	Cumin (jintan)
1/4 tsp	Coriander (ketumbar)
3-4	Lemon leaves (jerukpurut)
1 tsp	Ginger (jahe)
1/2 tsp	Kurkumaplant (kunyit)
1 Cup	Hot water
1/2 tsp	Sugar

✾ To prepare fish, combine salt and tamarind with enough water to form a paste. Rub the fish with this paste and let marinate 15-20 minutes. Meanwhile, using a wok set on medium heat, melt the butter and sauté the garlic, red chili and scallions for a few minutes. Add the cumin, coriander, lemon leaves, ginger and kurkumaplant.Let simmer for an additional 2-3 minutes. Add hot water and sugar. Add the fish, cover pan and let simmer for 15 minutes. Check the water level often, adding additional hot water as necessary so that fish is served in a sauce.

Mangut-Ikan
SPICED FISH

Chef's Notes:
Serve this spicy fish with white rice, summer vegetables, krupuk, sambal(s) of your choice and always with a cucumber salad.

1 1/2 lb	Cod or mackerel
2 tbsp	Butter
3-4	Scallions, minced
1	Clove garlic, minced
2	Red chilies, minced
5	Almond nuts (minced)
1/2 tsp	Kurkumaplant powder (kunyit)
2 inches	Kencur (can substitute w/ginger root or galangal root)
1/2 tsp	Shrimp paste (trassi)
	Salt, to taste
Dash	Sugar
1/2 tsp	Tamarind (asam) mixed w/ enough water to form a paste (or can use tamarind jelly)
8 oz	Coconut milk
3-4	Lemon leaves (jeruk purut)

✳ In a 350° oven, bake fish until completely done. Remove from oven and set aside. In wok, set on medium heat, melt butter and sauté the scallions, garlic, red chilies, almond nuts, kurkumaplant, kencur and shrimp paste for 2-3 minutes. Add salt, sugar and tamarind and continue simmering for 5 minutes. Add the coconut milk and lemon leaves and simmer, uncovered, for 2 minutes. Add the cooked fish and simmer again for 8 minutes or until done. Be careful not to over cook the fish. The fish should remain in one piece and served in a thick sauce.

Ikan Lombok
FOUR ALARM FISH
(IN A SPICY LOMBOK SAUCE)

Chef's Notes:
This dish is definitely not for the dinner guest with a tender palette. However, it is extremely simple to prepare and offers a quick way to dress up your left-over takeout from the night before. Serve either hot or cold with white rice, Sayur Asam (tamarind soup), cucumber salad and krupuk.

3	Fried fish portions (haddock or scrod is preferable)
10	Small red chilies, unseeded & minced
6	Red onions, minced
	Salt, to taste
1/2 tbsp	Coconut oil
1/2 Cup	Hot water
	Juice of 1 lemon (can substitute with 1 tbsp vinegar)

❋ To prepare sauce, crush together the red chilies, onion and salt. In wok, set on medium heat, heat the coconut oil. Add the crushed ingredients and sauté for 5 minutes. Add hot water, lemon juice (or vinegar) and let simmer for 5 minutes. Serve fish on a platter and pour sauce over the fish.

Ikan Kuning & Santan
FILLET OF HADDOCK IN A COCONUT SAUCE

Chef's Notes:
The coconut milk lends a sweet and creamy flavor to the haddock fillet. Serve with white rice and a vegetable of choice.

2-3	Cloves garlic, minced
	Salt, to taste
1/4 tsp	Cumin (jintan)
1/4 tsp	Shrimp paste (trassi)
1/2 tsp	Kurkumaplant powder (kunyit)
2 tbsp	Butter
1 1/2 lb	Haddock fillet, uncooked
1/2 tsp	Tamarind (asam)
8 oz	Coconut milk
1/2 tsp	Coriander seed (ketumbar)

✳ In wok or skillet, set on medium heat, sauté the garlic, salt, cumin, shrimp paste and kurkuma plant in butter for 2-3 minutes. Reduce heat. Add fish and let simmer 5-10 minutes, turning fish once so that it is browned on both sides. Add tamarind, coconut milk and coriander and continue simmering for a few more minutes, being careful not to over cook the fish. (fish should remain in one piece).

Frikadel Udang
INDONESIAN SHRIMP PATTIES

Chef's Notes:	8 oz — Small cooked shrimp, minced
Serve these tasty shrimp patties with white rice,	2 — Slices white bread, crusts removed
Sambal Telor, (hot sautéed eggs), Sambal	1 tbsp — Milk
Goreng Boontjes, (hot sautéed green beans).	2 — Egg yolks

8 oz	Small cooked shrimp, minced
2	Slices white bread, crusts removed
1 tbsp	Milk
2	Egg yolks
2	Egg whites
	Salt, to taste
	Pepper, to taste
Dash	Nutmeg
1	Leek, finely minced
3	Sprigs soup celery
	Bread crumbs
1 stick	Butter

❀ In mixing bowl, mince shrimp. Set aside. In separate bowl, combine white bread with milk and lightly toss until bread becomes soft. Add the shrimp, egg yolk, half of the egg whites (reserving the rest), salt, pepper, nutmeg, leek and celery. Mix thoroughly. Using your hands, make hamburger-sized patties. Dip the patties in the left-over egg whites and then roll in the bread crumbs, being sure to coat each side. Using a large skillet, cook the patties in browned-butter *until completely done.

***Heat butter in skillet until butter is a light-golden brown.**

RICE, NOODLES AND POTATOES

Rice is an essential part of the Indonesian's cuisine. It is served at dinner with meat, vegetables or fish. With a few simple herbs and spices, a plain dish can be transformed into something spectacular. In Indonesia, rice is regarded as a symbol of bounty. To this day, on the island of Java, villagers still give offerings of food and flowers to their rice goddess. Rice has become an essential part of society in the west as well. Until recently, due to its ill effect on birds, no western wedding was considered complete until rice was thrown at the exiting bride and groom. Today rice at weddings have been substituted with either flower petals or bird seeds. Before making any rice dish, please refer to the "The Right Tools For The Job", and "Rice" in the" Rice Table" chapter. It will provide information on making perfect rice, every time.

Noodles have become an important part of Indonesia's cuisine as well. This is due to the influence of the Chinese and the recipe, Bahmi, is a good example of this.

Potatoes, by themselves, would not be served to a guest in Indonesia. This would be a symbol of disrespect. They are considered to be very ordinary and therefore are eaten by ordinary people. There are a few exceptions, though. A dish like Timus (Baked Mashed Potatoes) is permitted when it is served with a variety of other dishes.

Nassi Kunjit
KURKUMAPLANT RICE

Chef's Notes:
This recipe offers a nice alternative to plain white rice. It is simple yet flavorful.

2 cups	Long grain white rice
1 cup	Coconut milk
3 cups	Water
1/2 tsp	Salt
2 tsp	Kurkumaplant Powder (kunyit)
1-2	Screw pine leaves (daun pan dan)
1 piece	Lemon grass (sereh) or 1/2 tsp powder
5	Lemon leaves (jeruk purut)

❋ Place uncooked rice in medium to large sauce pan. Combine coconut milk, water, salt, kurkuma plant, screw pine leaves, lemon grass and lemon leaves and pour over rice. Stir. Bring to a boil, reduce heat and let simmer until rice is completely cooked. (about 20 minutes). Remove from heat. Fluff with fork and serve.

Simple Nassi-Goreng
QUICK AND EASY INDONESIAN FRIED RICE

Chef's Notes:
In Indonesia, this recipe would be used for family, only. This should never be served to guests.

2 cups	Long grain white rice (or enough for 4 people)
2	Scallions, minced
2 tbsp	Butter
2	Eggs, beaten
Dash	Salt
	Aromat to taste (Maggi Dutch soy sauce)

✸ In large saucepan, cook rice until done. Set aside and let cool completely. In Wok, sauté the scallions in butter for 2 minutes. Add beaten eggs and scramble until eggs are fully cooked. Add cooled rice and simmer 2 minutes. Add salt and Aromat. Stir, mixing completely, and let simmer 5 minutes.

Rice, Noodles and Potatoes

Bahmi/ Ayan
CHICKEN WITH NOODLES

Chef's Notes:
There are those who say that Mie (Chinese noodles) and spaghetti are the same thing. However, I disagree. I feel that the two differ greatly in taste. Therefore, to preserve the integrity of this dish, you should make every attempt to use Mie. However, if this is impossible spaghetti can be used as a substitute.

2	Chicken breasts, cubed
3-4	Chicken livers, cubed
2 Cups	Water/chicken stock
2 tbsp	Butter
4	Cloves garlic, minced
4	Scallions, minced
1/2 tsp	Shrimp paste (trassi)
1 1/2 tsp	Ginger powder (jahe)
1 tsp	Salt
1/2 tsp	Pepper
1/2 tsp	Java sugar (gula jawa)
2 tbsp	Kecap
3	Sprigs soup celery, minced
2	Small leeks (cut into small rings)
1 cup	Pea pods (fresh)
1	Small head of cabbage, shredded
16 oz	Mie (Chinese noodles), or can substitute with spaghetti
1-2	Onions, sautéed

❋ Boil chicken breasts and livers in water until fully cooked. Remove and set aside, reserving 2 cups of the chicken stock. Let the chicken cool and then cut into small bite-sized pieces. Set aside.

❋ In Wok, sauté in butter the garlic, scallions, shrimp paste and ginger powder for 2-3 minutes.

❋ Add salt, pepper, java sugar, kecap, chicken and chicken stock. Stir and simmer for 2-3 minutes. Add soup celery, leek, pea pods. Simmer for a few more minutes. Add cabbage and cook until all vegetables are tender-crisp.

❋ In separate pot, boil noodles until fully cooked. Drain and add to the vegetables. Stir carefully, remove from heat, and serve.

Serving Suggestions:
Serve with sautéed onion sprinkled on top.

Rice, Noodles and Potatoes

Nasi Goreng II
INDONESIAN FRIED RICE

Chef's Notes:

This recipe is similar to the Nasi Goreng I, but imparts more flavor, due to the pork and smoked ham. If served with a salad, this makes a full meal.

2 cups	Long-grain white rice, cooked and cooled
8 oz.	Pork, cut into cubes
2 oz.	Smoked ham, sliced
3	Small onions, diced or 4 scallions, diced
1 Bag	Bumbu Nasi Goreng
2-3	Eggs
	Oil or butter

❀ Using a wok, sauté pork until half done. Add onions (or scallions) and Nasi Goreng spices. Stir and reduce heat to simmer. Continue simmering until pork is completely cooked. Add cooled rice and stir continually until everything is heated through.

❀ In separate skillet, make an omelet. Slice omelet into long, narrow pieces. Set aside. Slice ham into long pieces. Set aside. On a large platter or pasta bowl, spread the Nasi Goreng mixture. Place the omelet and ham slices on top, crosswise.

Rice, Noodles and Potatoes

Nassi Guri
FRAGRANT RICE

Chef's Notes:
Its title describes this recipe perfectly. You will love the odor that will fill your kitchen while you're preparing this dish.

2 cups	Long grain white rice
1 cup	Coconut Milk
2	Screw Pine leaves (daun pan dan)
2	Bay leaves (daun salam)
1	Lemon grass (sereh) or 1/2 tsp powder
5	Lemon leaves (jeruk purut)
1/2 tsp	Salt
	Water

✸ Rinse rice and place in medium-sized pot. Combine coconut milk with screw pine leaves, bay leaves, lemon grass, lemon leaves and salt. Pour coconut milk mixture over rice. Add enough water to cover the rice 1 inch. Stir. Bring to a boil, reduce heat to low and simmer, covered, until rice is completely cooked. (approximately 20 minutes). Remove from heat and fluff with fork.

Rice, Noodles and Potatoes

INDONESIAN FRIED RICE W/ OMELET

Chef's Notes:
This is a perfect dish to make using any left over meat such as steak, roast, pork or chicken. Serve with different sambals, a cucumber salad and kecap.

2 cups	Long-grain white rice
4	Cloves garlic, minced
4	Scallions, minced
4	Red chilies (red hot peppers), minced
3 tbsp	Butter
1/2 tsp	Shrimp paste (trassi)
1/2 tsp	Salt
1 cup	Meat, cooked and cut into cubes
1/2 Cup	Shrimp, cooked
3	Sprigs soup celery, minced
	Kecap, to taste
3	Eggs
1	Leek, sliced in rings

❀ Cook rice until done. Set aside and let cool completely. Fluff with fork.

❀ In wok, set on med/high heat, sauté garlic, scallions and pepper in butter for a few minutes stir ring constantly. Add shrimp paste, salt, meat and shrimp. Stir and let cook 2 minutes.

❀ Add cooked rice, stir and reduce heat to low. Add celery and leek. Continually stir, until all ingredients are heated through and vegetables are cooked but crisp. Add kecap, (to taste), set aside.

Omelet:

❀ Beat eggs, add 2 tbsp of milk, salt and pepper (to taste). Stir. In separate skillet, using butter or oil, make omelet. Use omelet for decoration and taste on top of the Nasi Goreng.

Krupuk: (Krupuk are wafers made out of shrimp, beef, etc.)

❀ In skillet, heat oil and fry large krupuk, one piece at a time until lightly browned. Remove and drain on brown paper bags. Serve on a separate platter.

Timus

STEWED POTATOES

(OR BAKED MASHED POTATOES)

Chef's Notes:
This dish can be cooked Au Bain Marie (using double boiler on the stove top). However, I prefer to bake it in the oven in a casserole dish with bread crumbs sprinkled on top.

10	Red Potatoes, unpeeled
1/2 Cup	Water
1/2 cup	Java Sugar (gula jawa)
3 tbsp	Pine Nuts
1/2 tsp	Salt
2 tbsp	Butter
	Bread crumbs (optional)

❁ Preheat oven to 350° In large pot, boil potatoes, unpeeled, until fully cooked. Remove from heat, drain, let cool and remove skins. Using a masher, mash potatoes and set aside. In separate pot, combine water, java sugar, pine nuts and salt and bring to a boil. Reduce heat and let simmer for 5 minutes. Remove mixture from heat, and combine with potatoes, mixing thoroughly. Poor entire mixture into a casserole dish. Cover with bread crumbs (optional) and bake at 350° until bread crumbs are lightly browned. (Approximately 30 - 40 minutes)

SOUPS AND SAUCES

There are so many nuances to the Indonesian culture and cuisine and none represents this better than the Indonesian Sops and Sayurs. The word Sayur by itself means Vegetables. However, when vegetables are cooked and prepared, as they are in the following chapter, they become sauces, gravies and even soups.

In many instances, the sayurs are used to accompany rice. They give moisture, as well as additional flavor, to what would have otherwise been a plain meal of white rice. They are also helpful for young children and the elderly, who need their foods softened to make them easier to chew.

My father preferred to eat them as soups - having them served on the side, as an accompaniment to his meal. However, there are a great many others who prefer to douse their rice in sayurs, creating, if you will, a "rice soup".

As you can see, it is hard to choose one word that specifically describes what Indonesian sops and sayurs are. Ultimately it is up to the person who is dining and what their particular preferences may be. In either case, they add vibrant flavor and texture to most any meal.

Guleh
LAMB SOUP

	Water
1 lb	Lamb meat, cut into bite-sized pieces
	Salt, to taste
2	Onions, minced
4	Cloves garlic, minced
2 tbsp	Butter
2 cups	Milk
2 tbsp	Shredded coconut
1 inch	Laos, grated or 1 tsp powder
1 tsp	Turmeric (kunyit)
1 tsp	Lemon grass powder (sereh) or 1 blade, fresh
1 tbsp	Sugar
1 tsp	Ground cloves
1 tsp	Cinnamon
1 tsp	Nutmeg
2 tbsp	Kecap
1 bunch	Soup celery, diced
1 lb	Cabbage, shredded
1/2 can	Green beans

Chef's Notes:
This soup can be served with white rice along with sambal, lemon slices and kecap.

❋ Place lamb in large pot and completely cover with water and salt, to taste. Bring to a boil, reduce heat and let simmer until half done. While lamb is cooking, sauté the onion, and garlic in butter for a few minutes, set aside.

❋ When meat is half done, add milk, coconut, laos, turmeric, lemon grass, sugar, cloves, cinnamon, nutmeg and kecap. Let simmer for 30 minutes. Add additional hot water as necessary to maintain a consistent fluid level. Add soup celery and sautéed onion and garlic. Add cabbage and green beans. Simmer until meat is completely cooked and tender.

Sajur Kim-loh
CHAMPIGNON SOUP
(MUSHROOM SOUP)

Chef's Notes:
This soup is not your ordinary mushroom soup.
The two varieties of Chinese champignons used
in this recipe give it an exotic flavor. They can
usually be purchased in Asian import stores and
in some large grocery stores.

1 lb	Beef poulet (soup or stew meat), cut into small pieces
4 cups	Cold water
1 oz	Shitake mushrooms
1 oz	Enoki mushrooms
4	Scallions, minced
3	Cloves garlic, minced
1/3 tsp	Shrimp paste (trassi)
1 tbsp	Butter
2	Leeks, cleaned and sliced into rings
2	Small bay leaves (daun salam)
1 tsp	Laos
	Salt, to taste
1/2 tsp	Pepper
1 tbsp	Kecap
1 cup	Bean sprouts
1 oz	Fresh Pea pods
1 tsp	Sugar

✻ Make beef stock by placing beef poulet in 4 cups of cold water. Bring to a boil and let simmer until fully cooked. Add the Shitake mushrooms and simmer 30 minutes. In wok, set on medium heat, sauté the scallions, garlic and shrimp paste in butter for 2-3 minutes. Add the leek, bay leaves, laos, salt and pepper and sauté for a few more minutes. Add the kecap and all of the sautéed ingredients to the soup. Simmer 8 more minutes. Add the bean sprouts, pea pods and sugar and simmer 1 minute, or until vegetables are tender-crisp. Add Enoki mushrooms to soup immediately before serving.

Sayur Currie Java
CURRIED JAVA SOUP

Chef's Notes:
This soup tastes wonderful when served with white rice, Goreng Timpi, (sautéed soy bean cakes), Lapjes Ayam (boned chicken fried in an egg batter), and a cucumber salad.

1 lb	Beef poulet, (stew meat) cut into bite-sized pieces
4 cups	Water
4	Scallions, finely minced
2	Cloves garlic, finely minced
1	Red chilie, finely minced (or 1 tbsp of any dried red pepper)
1 tbsp	Ginger (jahe)
1 tsp	Turmeric (kunyit)
1 tbsp	Coriander (ketumbar)
1/2 tsp	Cumin (jintan)
1 tsp	Shrimp paste (trassi)
2 tbsp	Butter
1	Lemon grass blade (sereh)
1	Large Bay leaf (daun salam)
1 cup	Green beans, diced
5	Potatoes, peeled and cut into bite-sized pieces
8 oz	Coconut milk
3	Bouillon cubes (beef or chicken flavor)
1/2 tsp	Sugar

❀ To create the beef stock, simmer meat in water for 1 hour. Meanwhile, in wok, set on medium heat, sauté the scallions, garlic, red chilies, ginger, turmeric, coriander, cumin and shrimp paste in butter for 3-4 minutes.

❀ Add the lemon grass and bay leaf and let simmer 2 minutes. Remove from heat, adding it to the beef stock and let simmer in the beef stock for a few minutes. Add the green beans and potatoes. Cover and simmer a few more minutes. Add the coconut milk, bouillon cubes and sugar. Simmer, uncovered, for 2-3 minutes or until vegetables are cooked.

Sayur Gudek
CHICKEN AND TROPICAL FRUIT SOUP

Chef's Notes:
This Indonesian recipe calls for 2 lbs of Nangka. Nangka is a jack fruit. It is a large, melon-shaped fruit with thick, green skin and yellow flesh with a bread-like texture. Unfortunately, it would be virtually impossible to find this fruit any where other than Indonesia. Therefore, you can substitute by using Mango.

1	Whole chicken
	Water
	Salt, to taste
2	Scallions, minced
2	Cloves garlic, minced
1 inch	Laos or 1 tsp powder
1	Large bay leaf (daun salam)
1	Large red chilie, unseeded & minced
1 tsp	Coriander (ketumbar)
1/2 tsp	Cumin (jintan)
1 tsp	Shrimp paste (trassi)
6-7	Almonds, minced
2 tbsp	Butter
2 lbs	Tropical fruit*, cleaned and cut into 1-inch pieces
2	Chicken-flavored bouillon cubes
8 oz	Coconut milk
1/4 tsp	Sugar

❋ To prepare, place chicken in a large pot and completely cover with cold, salted water. Bring to a boil, reduce heat and simmer until chicken is completely cooked. Remove chicken from pot, reserving the bouillon. Remove the chicken from the bone, (discarding the bones),cut meat into bite-sized pieces and return chicken pieces to the bouillon. In wok, set on medium heat, sauté the scallions, garlic, laos, bay leaf, red chilie, coriander, cumin, shrimp paste and almonds in butter for 2-3 minutes. Add the sautéed ingredients to the bouillon and let simmer for a few minutes. Add the tropical fruit, bouillon cubes, coconut milk and sugar, and simmer for at least a half hour, uncovered. Fruit should be well done. Be sure to check water level often, adding additional hot water as necessary to maintain consistent fluid level.

See Chef's Notes.

Sayur Menir
SPINACH SOUP

Chef's Notes:
I like to serve this soup with Babi Kecap (pork in a kecap sauce). However, it is just as good when served with your favorite chicken or meat dish along with white rice, Sambal Goreng Telor (hot sautéed eggs) and krupuk.

4 cups	Beef stock
2	Large onions or 4 scallions, minced
1 1/2	Cloves garlic, minced
1/2 tsp	Shrimp paste (trassi)
1	Arromated root (temu kunci)
1/2 tsp	Coriander (ketumbar)
1	Cucumber, peeled and sliced into thick slices
1 1/2	Beef-flavored bouillon cubes
1 can	Whole kernel corn
16 oz	Fresh spinach, rinsed
1/2 tsp	Sugar

✿ Make beef stock by cooking pieces of beef in 2 cups of cold water and letting simmer. To this add the onions (or scallions), garlic, shrimp paste, arromated root and coriander. Simmer 8 minutes. Add the cucumber slices, bouillon cubes and corn. Let simmer for a few minutes. Add the spinach and sugar. Stir and let simmer for 2-3 minutes or until the spinach and cucumber are cooked, but crisp.

Sayur Pindang Kuning
TANGY MEAT SOUP

Chef's Notes:
Serve this soup with any meal that needs a little zest. It also tastes great when served over white rice.

1 tsp	Laos
1	Lemon grass blade (sereh), or
	1 tsp powder
1	Large bay leaf (daun salam)
1/2 tsp	Turmeric (kunyit)
1/2 tsp	Shrimp paste (trassi)
3	Beef-flavored bouillon cubes
11/2 cups	Green beans, cut in half
2 tbsp	Sugar
1/2 Head	Savoy cabbage, shredded
2 tbsp	Tamarind (asam)

✺ In large pot, simmer meat in 4 cups of cold water until mostly cooked. In wok, sauté scallions, red chilies and garlic in butter for a few minutes. To this add laos, lemon grass, bay leaf, turmeric and shrimp paste. Stir and let simmer 2 minutes. Add the sautéed ingredients to the soup, along with the bouillon cubes. Stir and let simmer, covered for 8 minutes. Add green beans, sugar, cabbage and tamarind. Simmer for a few minutes or until beans are tender crisp.

Meat Dishes

TAHU AND TIMPI
(SOY BEAN CAKES)

Tahu and timpi are a dieters dream. They are filling, versatile, very nutritious and, best of all, low fat. The tahu, which is more widely known as tofu, is made from bean curd. The timpi (or sometimes spelled tempe) are made from fermented soy beans and have a bit more texture than their cousin, the tofu. Because they lack any real flavor of their own, they can be used in most any dish and easily adopt the flavor of the spices used in any given recipe.

For a delicious snack, try the Oblok Oblok Kemiri recipe in this chapter. It is very healthy. It can also be used as a side dish with any of the sayurs from the previous chapter.

Tumis Tahu with Toge and Udang
SHRIMP AND TOFU IN A HOT SAUCE

Chef's Notes:
This will make a complete and tasty meal when served with white rice, krupuk and a cucumber salad.

1	Tofu cake (tahu), medium texture, cut into 1-inch squares
1/2 cup	Virgin olive oil
1	Red paprika, cut into small pieces
1	Green paprika, cut into small pieces
3	Cloves garlic, finely minced
4	Scallions, finely minced
1/2 tsp	Tamarind (asam) mixed w/enough water to form a paste (or can use tamarind jelly)
1/4 tsp	Salt
1/2 tsp	Shrimp paste (trassi)
2 tbsp	Butter
1/2 inch	Laos or 1/2 tsp powder
1	Large bay leaf (daun salam)
1 cup	Boiling water
1 cup	Bean sprouts, rinsed, drained and soaked in hot water for 2 minutes
1 tbsp	Sugar
6 stalks	Soup celery, finely sliced
1 cup	Small cooked shrimp
1 Large	Leek cut into rings

❋ Heat the olive oil in a wok set on high heat. Add the tofu and sauté until light brown. Drain and arrange tofu pieces on a platter. Set aside. Combine the red and green pepper, garlic, scallions, tamarind, salt and shrimp paste and using wok, sauté in butter for 2-3 minutes. Add the laos, bay leaf and boiling water. Simmer a few minutes and add the bean sprouts and sugar. Add the celery, shrimp, tofu and leek and continue simmering for 2-3 minutes. Be sure to check the water level often, adding additional hot water as necessary so that tofu is served in a sauce.

Soy Bean Cakes

Tahu Ketoprak
SAUTÉED TOFU WITH RAW VEGETABLES

Chef's Notes:
Satay sauce can be used in lieu of the Kecap Sauce. (or you can use both.) Serve with white rice, any fish dish, fresh cucumbers and Krupuk Ikan, (fish crackers).

1	Tofu cake (tahu) firm
3 tbsp	Extra virgin olive oil
1 cup	Bean Sprouts
1/2 head	Chinese cabbage
3 sprigs	Soup celery, finely minced
2	Salad onions, finely minced

Kecap Sauce:

1/2 tsp	Salt
1/2 tsp	Java sugar (gula jawa)
1/2 tsp	Shrimp paste (trassi)
4 tbsp	Kecap manis (Indonesian soy sauce)
2 tbsp	Lemon juice
3	Cloves garlic, finely minced
3	Scallions finely minced
3	Red chillies, unseeded and minced
2	Large onions, sautéed (or dry roasted)

✳ Cut tofu into 1-inch squares. Place in colander to drain. Set aside. Heat olive oil in wok until oil is very hot. Sauté the tofu by arranging the tofu, piece by piece, in the oil. Sauté the tofu until light brown. Drain and arrange on a platter. Boil the bean sprouts in water for a few minutes, or until tender crisp. Drain and set aside. Slice cabbage in long thin slices, rinse, drain and set aside.

✳ *To prepare the kecap sauce:* Mash together the salt, sugar, shrimp paste, kecap and lemon juice. To this, add the garlic, scallions, and red chillies. Put in a small glass bowl and set aside.

✳ *To serve:* Arrange a few pieces of tofu on a plate. Sprinkle with bean sprouts, cabbage, celery and salad onion. Pour the kecap sauce over this and top off with either sautéed or dry roasted onions.

Soy Bean Cakes

Oblok Oblok Kemiri
ALMOND NUT CAKES

Chef's Notes:	

Chef's Notes:
When purchasing your tofu, try to buy the extra firm kind. As tofu breaks apart easily, especially during cooking, be extra careful when stirring. If the amount of hot peppers listed in the ingredients intimidates you, you can certainly adjust them to your taste.

1	Soy bean flour cake (timpi)
1	Tofu cake (tahu), firm
4	Cloves garlic, minced
3	Red chilies, unseeded and minced
4	Green chilies, unseeded and minced
6	Scallions, minced
1/2 tsp	Cumin (jintan)
1 tsp	Coriander (ketumbar)
1 1/2 tsp	Salt
1 1/2 tsp	Tamarind (asam) mixed w/enough water to form a paste (or can use tamarind jelly)
8	Almond nuts, crushed
4	Small bay leaves (daun salam)
2 tsp	Java sugar (gula jawa)
2 tsp	Shrimp paste (trassi)
1 tsp	Laos or 1 inch of the laos root
2 tbsp	Butter
2 1/2 cups	Boiling water
8 oz	Coconut milk

❁ Cut soy bean cake and tofu cake into 2-inch pieces. Place in colander and let drain. Set aside. In wok, set on medium heat, sauté the garlic, red and green chilies, scallions, cumin, coriander, salt, tamarind, almond nuts, bay leaves, java sugar, shrimp paste and laos in butter for 2-3 minutes. Add 2 1/2 cups of boiling water, stir and let simmer, covered, for 5 minutes. Add the tofu and con tinue simmering, covered, for a few more minutes. Add the coconut milk and the soy bean flour cake. Simmer, uncovered, for 5 minutes. Check the water level often, adding additional hot water as necessary so that dish is served in a sauce.

Soy Bean Cakes

Tahu Goreng Telor
TOFU OMELETS WITH A SWEET AND SOUR SAUCE

Chef's Notes:
Tahu Goreng Telor can be served as a main dish or as a side dish. Serve with white rice, krupuk and a cucumber salad.

Omelets:

1	Tofu cake (tahu), firm
4	Small eggs, lightly beaten
	Juice of 2 Cloves of garlic
1/4 tsp	Aromat (Dutch soy sauce)
1/8 tsp	Nutmeg
1 tbsp	Flour
	Butter or oil

Sauce:

3	Red chilies, minced
1	Clove garlic, minced
2	Scallions, minced
1/4 tsp	Shrimp paste (trassi)
1/4 tsp	Salt
1 tbsp	Butter
1/2 tsp	Petis (fish/shrimp paste)
5 tbsp	Kecap
1/2 tsp	Java sugar (gula jawa)
	Juice of 1 lemon
1/2 head	White cabbage, finely minced
1 bunch	Soup celery, finely minced

✸ *To Prepare Tofu:* Cut tofu into 1-inch pieces. Place in a colander to drain. Heat small amount of oil in wok, brown Tofu on all sides. Set aside.

✸ *To Prepare Omelets:* In mixing bowl, combine the eggs with the garlic juice, aromat, nutmeg and flour. Mix thoroughly. Using butter or oil in a heated skillet, make 5 omelets.

✸ *To prepare the sauce:* Combine red chilies, garlic, scallions, shrimp paste and salt and using a wok, sauté in butter for 2-3 minutes. Combine the petis, kecap and sugar and add to the wok. Stir. Add the lemon juice, stir and let simmer for a few minutes.

✸ *To serve:* Place omelets on individual plates, cover with cabbage, celery, and tofu and top with the sauce.

Soy Bean Cakes

EGGS—NOT JUST FOR BREAKFAST ANYMORE

Due to the Indonesians' affinity for spices, the egg dishes that are represented on the next few pages can in no way be confused with the normal serving of breakfast. Eggs, which are generally made into omelets, make for the perfect appetizer or accompaniment to a variety of dishes, such as Rice, Salads, Soups, Krupuk (shrimp crackers) and Sambal Goreng Boontjes (Hot and Spicy Green Beans). They also go well with soups, such as Sayur Menir, (Spinach Soup). Or the cook may choose to serve them as a main course, for which they are certainly hardy enough.

Dadar Jamur
CHAMPIGNON OMELET
(MUSHROOM OMELET)

Chef's Notes:
This recipe calls for browned flour. To do this, add flour to a heated pan, with no oil. Stir quickly and constantly until flour becomes a light brown then immediately remove from heat.

4	Eggs, beaten
1/4 tsp	Salt
1/8 tsp	Nutmeg
1 cup plus 4 tbsp	Milk
1/2 tsp	Pepper
2 tbsp	Butter
1 cup	Champignons (mushrooms)
1	Scallion, finely minced
2 tbsp	Water
2 tbsp	Browned flour*
	Juice of half a lemon
1/4 tsp	Aromat (Dutch soy sauce)

✼ Mix eggs with salt, nutmeg, 4 tbsp milk and pepper. Using a skillet set on medium heat, melt 1 tbsp of butter and make 2 to 4 omelets. Set aside. Cut champignons into thin slices. Using a wok, sauté the champignons and the scallions in 1 tbsp of butter for 2 minutes. Add 2 tbsp water, simmer 5 minutes. Add the browned flour*, stir. Add the milk, lemon juice and aromat. Stir and let simmer another 5 minutes or until mixture begins to thicken. If necessary, add salt, to taste.

✼ *To serve:* Place omelets on a warm platter. Fill omelets with the champignon mixture and fold over.

* See Chef's Notes.

Dadar Jawa
MOM'S VEGETABLE OMELETS

Chef's Notes:
These are the omelets that my mother made for me as a child. They are quick and easy but are full of flavor. Serve with white rice, your choice of sayur, satay, krupuk, and your choice of sambal(s).

2	Eggs
2 tbsp	Water
1 tbsp	Leek, finely minced
1/2 tsp	Onion, finely minced
1/2 tsp	Red chilies, finely minced (or sambal ulek)
1 tsp	Celery, finely minced
Dash	Nutmeg
Dash	Salt, to taste
2 tbsp	Butter

✱ Blend eggs and water together in a bowl. Add the leek, onion, red chilli, celery, nutmeg and salt, mixing thoroughly. In skillet, heat butter and make 4 omelets.

Telor Isi
OMELET WITH BEEF AND COCONUT FILLING

Chef's Notes:
The ground beef and coconut combined with the vegetables and spices make this omelet hardy-enough to be served at any meal.

Omelet:

4	Eggs
1/4 tsp	Aromat (Dutch soy sauce)
Dash	Nutmeg
Dash	Sugar
1-2 tbsp	Butter

Filling:

2 cup	Ground beef
2 tbsp	Butter
1	Small leek, finely minced
5 sprigs	Soup celery, finely minced
2-3	Scallions, finely minced
1	Red chilie, minced
1 tsp	Curry
1 tbsp	Shredded coconut
	Salt, to taste

❀ Combine eggs, aromat, nutmeg and sugar. Melt butter in skillet set on medium heat and make 4 omelets. Set aside, keeping omelets warm by placing omelets on a platter and set on top of a pan filled with hot water.

❀ *To prepare filling:* Sauté ground meat, with 2 tbsp of butter, in wok set on medium heat. Let simmer for a few minutes. Add the remainder of the ingredients and continue simmering until meat is completely cooked.

❀ *To serve:* Place omelets on a warmed platter, spread filling on omelet and fold over.

Orak Arik Udang/Daging
STIR-FRIED SHRIMP OR MEAT WITH EGGS

Chef's Notes:
If you do not have shrimp available, this dish offers the perfect opportunity to use up any left over meat.

1/2 lb	Cooked shrimp (or any cooked left over meat)
1/2 lb	Green beans or cabbage
4	Red onions, thinly sliced
2	White onions, thinly sliced
2 tbsp	Virgin olive oil
	Salt, to taste
	Pepper, to taste
4	Eggs, beaten
	Parsley, chopped

❋ Mince shrimp (or other meat). Set aside. Slice green beans (or cabbage) into thin pieces. Set aside. In wok, set on medium heat, sauté onions in oil until onions begin to turn light brown. Add shrimp (or meat), stir. Add green beans (or cabbage), salt and pepper. Continue cooking until cabbage is fully cooked. (Check cabbage often for doneness). Add eggs and stir constantly until eggs are fully cooked, (about 2 minutes). Garnish with some parsley sprinkled on top.

Dadar Bumbu
INDONESIAN VEGETABLE OMELET

Chef's Notes:
This recipe is the Indonesian equivalent of the Breakfast Burrito.

4	Eggs, beaten
2	Red chilies, unseeded and finely minced
1-1 1/2	Cloves garlic, finely minced
2	Scallions, finely minced
1/4 tsp	Shrimp paste (trassi)
	Salt, to taste
4 sprigs	Soup celery, finely minced
1	Small leek, finely minced
Dash	Sugar
	Butter or virgin olive oil

❀ In glass bowl, beat the eggs. To this add the peppers, garlic and scallions, stir. Add shrimp paste and salt. Stir. Add the celery, leek and dash of sugar and mix thoroughly. Melt butter (or heat oil) in skillet and make 2 to 4 omelets. Serve on a hot platter, rolled up like burritos.

Egg Dishes

Kari Telur
CURRIED EGGS IN THE ROUND

Chef's Notes:
It is customary in my family to serve this recipe, as well as all of the egg recipes in this chapter, on a heated plate or platter. This can be done by placing the serving platter on top of a pan filled with boiling water or placing the platter in a 200° oven for a few minutes.

2 cups	Any quality white rice
2 tbsp	Butter
2	Onions minced
3 tsp	Curry powder (or to taste)
2 tbsp	Flour mixed w/water to form paste
2 cups	Hot chicken stock (or water mixed w/ 3 chicken-flavored bouillon cubes)
1/2 cup	Milk
	Salt, to taste
	Pepper, to taste
5	Eggs, hard boiled and cut in half
4	sprigs Fresh parsley, finely chopped

❀ Boil rice according to package instructions. Set aside.

❀ To prepare the sauce: Using a wok, set on medium heat, melt butter. To this add the onion and curry. Stir continuously until onions are half done. Add the flour paste, stir. Gradually add the chicken stock, stirring constantly. Add the milk, salt, and pepper. Simmer 7 minutes, stirring constantly.

❀ To serve: Use a round cake pan, rinsed with hot water. Press the cooked rice into the sides of the cake pan, forming a ring. Turn pan over onto a round, hot platter*. Arrange the half-cut eggs around the outside of the rice ring. Pour the sauce inside the ring and over the rice and eggs. Sprinkle chopped parsley as a garnish.

***See Chef's Notes.**

Egg Dishes

SALADS AND VEGETABLES

Indonesia's topography is varied and abundant. Therefore, they are able to produce a large variety of vegetables and fruit. Tropically grown vegetables are cultivated on the lower elevations. Whereas, cabbage, leek, snow peas, cauliflower, etc., are grown in the higher elevations. What a delicacy of choices!

Everything is purchased on a daily basis and consumed that day. You can not get any fresher.

Acar Biet
BEET SALAD WITHOUT ONIONS

Chef's Notes:
This salad goes great with hamburgers. It's a great alternative to french fries and certainly more healthful.

6-8	Beets, fully cooked
1 qt	Cold water
1 1/2 tsp	Salt
4 1/2 tbsp	Sugar
10-12	Black peppercorns
6	Whole cloves
4-5 tbsp	White vinegar

✽ Cut cooked beets into 1/8 inch slices, set aside. In wok, bring 1 quart of cold water to a boil. Add salt, sugar, peppercorns and cloves. Add beets and vinegar. Reduce heat and let simmer for a few minutes. Remove from heat and let cool. Store in a tight, non-metallic container.

Salads and Vegetables

Acar Biet
BEET SALAD WITH ONIONS

Chef's Notes:
This is a versatile salad that can be served as a hot relish dish or as a cold salad. Serve with ground meat, chicken, krupuk and your choice of sambals.

6-8	Beets, fully cooked
1 qt	Cold water
1 1/2 tsp	Salt
4 1/2 tsp	Sugar
10-12	Black peppercorns
6	Whole cloves
4-5 tbsp	White vinegar
1	Large onion, minced
1 tbsp	Butter
2 tbsp	Cornstarch

❀ Cut cooked beets into 1/8 inch slices, set aside. In wok, bring 1 quart of cold water to a boil. Add salt, sugar, peppercorns and cloves. Add beets and vinegar. Reduce heat and let simmer for a few minutes. Sauté onion in butter until light brown. Add the sautéed onion to the beet mixture and return to a boil. Add corn starch that has been mixed with enough water to form a paste. Continue boiling until sauce thickens, remove from heat.

Semoor Terung
SIMMERED EGGPLANT

Chef's Notes:	4 Small eggplants
Serve this dish with white rice, krupuk, Sambal	3 tbsp Butter
Goreng Daging (hot sautéed meat), satay and/or	1 cup Hot water
your choice of meat dish.	1-2 Cloves garlic, minced
	2-3 tbsp Kecap manis (sweet soy sauce)
	3-4 Scallions, minced
	2 Small cloves
	Dash Pepper
	Dash Nutmeg
	1 Chicken-flavored bouillon cube
	1/2 tsp Sugar

❋ Rinse eggplants, cut off ends and cut lengthwise into large pieces. Using a large skillet, set on medium heat, sauté the eggplants in butter until brown. Remove from skillet and set aside. Using the same pan, add hot water, garlic, kecap and scallions. Simmer 3-4 minutes. Add cloves, pepper, nutmeg and bouillon cube. Simmer 3-4 minutes. Return eggplant to skillet, add sugar, cover and simmer for 5 minutes. Serve on an attractive platter.

Salads and Vegetables

Urap
VEGETABLES WITH SHREDDED COCONUT

Chef's Notes:
Serve with white rice, fried fish and your choice of chicken dish.

1 cup	Blanched green beans*, diced
1 cup	Bean sprouts, rinsed and drained
1 head	Cabbage, shredded
1-2	Cucumbers, peeled, unseeded and cut into 1-inch pieces
2-3	Red chilies, unseeded and minced
2	Scallions, minced
2	Cloves garlic, minced
1/2 tsp	Salt
1/2 tsp	Java sugar (gula jawa)
1/2 tsp	Tamarind (asam)
1 tsp	Shrimp paste (trassi)
6	Kencur (a root similar to ginger and galingale)
5	Lemon leaves (jeruk purut)
3/4 cup	Shredded coconut
2	Bay leaves (daun salam)
1 tbsp	Lemon juice

❀ Combine green beans, bean sprouts, cabbage and cucumber in a bowl and set aside. In small bowl, crush together the red chilies, scallions and garlic. Add salt, java sugar, tamarind, shrimp paste, kencur and lemon leaves. Set aside. Using wok, set on medium heat, simmer coconut and bay leaves together for a few minutes, stirring constantly (do not use any water or oil, coconut will produce slight moisture when heated). Add all of the crushed ingredients and continue stir ring constantly until coconut becomes a light brown color. Add vegetables, stir. Add lemon juice, reduce heat to low, and continue simmering for a few minutes.

* To Blanch – Drop vegetables into boiling water and let cook for about one minute.
Remove from heat and drain.

Salads and Vegetables

Gado-Gado
STEAMED VEGETABLES WITH PEANUT BUTTER SAUCE

Chef's Notes:
Please don't let the amount of ingredients listed deter you from creating this dish. Although it can be intimidating, it is not as difficult as it looks and once prepared, makes for a delicious meal and a stunning presentation.

1/2 head	Cabbage, shredded
1/2 head	Cauliflower, broken into bite-sized pieces
1 cup	Whole green beans
1 head	Romaine lettuce, torn into large pieces
1	Cucumber, sliced
	Salt, to taste
2 cups	Bean sprouts
1	Tofu cake (tahu) cut into bite-sized pieces
1	Timpi (soy bean cake) cut into bite-sized pieces
6 tbsp	Oil
2-3	Scallions, minced
2	Cloves garlic, minced
2-3	Red chilies, unseeded and minced
1/2 tsp	Shrimp paste (trassi)
1/4 tsp	Laos
1 tsp	Tamarind (asam) mixed w/enough water to make a thin paste (or can use tamarind jelly)
2	Lemon leaves (jeruk purut)
1 cup	Peanut butter
8 oz	Coconut milk
1 tbsp	Java sugar (gula jawa)
3-4	Medium-sized potatoes, boiled, cooled and sliced
4	Hard boiled eggs, sliced
1 jar	Baby Corn

❀ Using a vegetable steamer, steam the rinsed cabbage, cauliflower, green beans and romaine lettuce until cooked, but crisp. Drain and set aside, letting cool completely. Slice cucumber and sprinkle with some salt. Set aside.Place bean sprouts in bowl and cover with hot water for 3 minutes. Drain and set aside, letting cool completely. Using wok, set on medium heat, sauté the tahu and timpi in 4 tbsp of oil until light brown. Drain and set aside.

❀ *To prepare the sauce:* Using wok, heat 2 tbsp of oil and sauté scallions, garlic, red chilies, shrimp paste, laos, tamarind and lemon leaves on low heat for 3 minutes. Add peanut butter and dash of salt. Stir. Add coconut milk and java sugar. Stir and let simmer for 10 minutes. Set aside and let cool. (If sauce is too thick, add a little bit of hot water or milk)

❀ *To serve:* Arrange vegetables and potatoes in layers on a large platter. Garnish with tahu, timpi and hard boiled eggs. Pour sauce over everything. (You can reserve some of the sauce to be served on the side).

Rujak
CURRANT SALAD

Chef's Notes:
This is an extremely simple salad to prepare. It is sweet and hot and makes for a unique appetizer or dessert.

1 1/2 cups	Currants
2 tbsp	Kecap
3 tbsp	Java Sugar (gula jawa)
1/2 tsp	Sambel Ulek (Indonesian hot pepper paste)

✹ Rinse currants, drain and set aside. Using a glass bowl, combine kecap, java sugar and sambal ulek. Add currants and stir. Cover and store in refrigerator until ready to serve. Salad should be served cold.

Rujak Petis
FRUIT SALAD WITH PETIS

Chef's Notes:
This salad can be used as an appetizer or as an after-dinner dessert.

3	Granny Smith apples
4	Cooking Pears
1	Cucumber
1/2 head	Cabbage
1	Pineapple (optional) fresh or canned
2	Red chilies, unseeded and minced
1 tsp	Tamarind (asam)
1/2 tsp	Shrimp paste (trassi)
2 tbsp	Petis (fish-shrimp paste)
1 tbsp	Kecap manis (sweet soy sauce)
1/2 tsp	Lemon juice

❋ Rinse the apples and pears well and cut into quarters. (Cut each fruit once lengthwise and once widthwise, so that there are four pieces). Set aside. Slice cucumber, length wise, (do not peel cucumber), set aside. Break apart cabbage into bite-sized pieces. Set aside. Cut pineapple into small pieces, set aside.

❋ *To prepare the sauce:* Crush red chilies, tamarind, shrimp paste and petis together. Add kecap and lemon juice and mix thoroughly, making a thin, paste-like sauce.

❋ *To Serve:* Arrange fruit and vegetables on an attractive platter and pour the sauce over all of the fruit and vegetables.

Jagung
SWEET CORN AND SHREDDED COCONUT

Chef's Notes:
This can be served hot or cold with Nassi Goreng (Indonesian fried rice) as a side dish.

5-6	Ears of corn or 3-4 small cans of corn
4 oz.	Shredded coconut
1/4 tsp	Salt
1 tbsp	Sugar

❋ Boil corn, unshucked (tastes better) for 15 minutes. Remove from heat, cool and shuck. Remove kernels by holding ear upright and using sharp knife to slice off kernels. Set aside. (If using canned corn, boil corn for 6 minutes, drain and then add corn to coconut).

❋ Heat wok and using a little oil quickly stir-fry the shredded coconut for 1 minute, stirring constantly. Add kernels, stir. Add salt and sugar and continue stirring until sugar caramelizes.

Rujak Manis
SWEET AND SOUR FRUIT SALAD

Chef's Notes:
If the apples are not tart enough or if you prefer a more sour fruit salad, you can adjust the tartness by adding lemon juice. For a change of pace, I like to use pineapple, in lieu of the pears. This salad can be prepared a day in advance.

3	Granny Smith apples
4	Cooking pears
1	Cucumber
1/2 head	Cabbage
1	Pineapple (optional) fresh or canned
2	Red chilies, unseeded and minced or
1 tsp	Sambal Ulek
2 tbsp	Java sugar (gula jawa)
1/2 tsp	Shrimp paste (trassi)
1 tsp	Tamarind (asam)
1/2 tsp	Salt
	Lemon juice, to taste (optional) *

❊ Rinse the apples and pears well and cut into 8 sections. (Cut each fruit once lengthwise and once widthwise, and then again width wise, so that there are eight pieces). Set aside. Slice cucumber, widthwise, slightly thicker than you would for a cucumber salad. (do not peel cucumber), set aside. Break apart cabbage into bite-sized pieces. Set aside. Cut pineapple into small pieces, set aside.

❊ *To prepare the sauce:* Crush red chilies, java sugar, shrimp paste, tamarind and salt together. Add some water and mix thoroughly, making a thin, paste-like sauce.

❊ *To Serve:* Arrange fruit and vegetables on an attractive platter and pour the sauce over all of the fruit and vegetables.

***See Chef's Notes.**

Papaja Manis
SWEET AND SOUR PAPAYA

Chef's Notes:
This recipe is extremely easy, but makes for a wonderful display when served in attractive cups. The brilliance of the yellow fruit adds color and elegance to any table.

1	Papaya
1 tbsp	Sugar
	Juice of half a lemon

❋ Peel Papaya and remove pit. Cut papaya into bite-sized pieces and place in a bowl. Sprinkle papaya with sugar and drizzle with the juice from the lemon. Toss lightly. Cover and store in refrigerator until ready to serve. Papaya should be served cold.

Acar Campur II
TOO-HOT-TO-HANDLE VEGETABLE SALAD

Chef's Notes:
I personally prefer this version of Acar Campur because of the intensity of flavor and texture the additional spices and ingredients imparts. Serve with white rice and any chicken, fish, or meat dish.

1 cup	Butterfly cabbage
1 cup	Green beans
1 cup	Carrots
1 cup	Bean sprouts
2	Red chilies, unseeded and minced
3-4	Whole green chilies, unseeded
2-3	Cloves garlic, minced
2-3	Scallions, minced
1-2 tbsp	Butter
3	Almonds, crushed
1/2 tsp	Java Sugar (gula jawa)
1/2 tsp	Shrimp paste (trassi)
1/2tsp	Ginger powder (jahe)
1 tsp	Turmeric (kunyit)
1-2 tbsp	Hot water
10	Small Spanish hot peppers (jalapeno)
3-4	Whole green chilies, unseeded
1/4 tsp	Salt
2-3 tbsp	White vinegar
2	Small bay leaves (daun salam)

✤ To prepare, cut cabbage, green beans and carrots into julienne strips. Rinse, separate vegetables by type and set aside. Rinse bean sprouts, drain and set aside. Remove seeds from red and green chilies. Mince only the red chili and set aside. In wok, set on medium heat, sauté the red chilies, garlic and scallions in butter for 2-3 minutes. Add the crushed almonds, java sugar, shrimp paste, ginger and turmeric. Add hot water and let simmer 3 minutes. Add carrots and green beans and simmer 1 minute. Add cabbage, bean sprouts, whole green chilies, jalapeno peppers, salt, vinegar and bay leaves. Stir and let simmer until all vegetables are cooked but tender crisp. Add additional hot water if necessary so that vegetables do not become too dry.

Salads and Vegetables

SAMBALS AND SAUCES
(HOT AND SPICY RELISHES
AND OTHER SAUCES)

Sambals are a staple item in any Indonesian's kitchen. They are the equivalent of the American's salt and pepper. The phrase, "a little goes a long way" explains this condiment perfectly for they are generally very spicy. When and how much are used is determined by the level of tolerance a person has for spice. Depending on the individual person's preferences, sambals can essentially be used as a garnish or accompaniment to almost any dish in this book. You may, however, want to keep the fire extinguisher near by.

Sambal Goreng Boontjes
HOT SAUTÉED GREEN BEANS

Chef's Notes:
Serve these spicy green beans with white rice, krupuk, and a cucumber salad.

2	Red chilies, unseeded and minced
3-4	Scallions, minced
1-1 1/2	Cloves garlic, minced
2 tbsp	Butter
	Salt, to taste
1/4 tsp	Tamarind (asam)
1 tsp	Shrimp paste (trassi)
1/2 lb	Small cooked shrimp or left over cooked meat cut into small pieces
1 lb	French cut beans, frozen
2	Small bay leaves (daun salam)
1 inch	Laos or 1 tsp powder
1/4 tsp	Coriander (ketumbar)
1/2 cup	Hot water
8 oz	Coconut milk
Dash	Sugar

❋ Combine the red chilies, scallions and garlic and using a wok sauté in butter for a few minutes. Add salt, tamarind and shrimp paste, simmer 2 minutes. Add the shrimp (or meat) and the beans, stir. Add the bay leaves, laos and coriander. Stir. Add hot water and let simmer, covered, for 8 minutes. Add the coconut milk and sugar and simmer uncovered until oil forms on top. If needed, add an additional 1/2 cup of hot water to maintain fluid level.

Sambal Goreng Udang
HOT SAUTEED SHRIMP

2	Red chilies, unseeded and minced
1-1 1/2	Cloves garlic, minced
4-5	Scallions, minced
1/4 tsp	Shrimp paste (trassi)
1/2 tsp	Tamarind (asam)
1/4 tsp	Salt
2 tbsp	Butter
1 piece	Lemon grass blade (sereh)
1	Small bay leaf (daun salam)
1/2 inch	Laos or 1/2 tsp powder
4	Lemon leaves (jerukpurut)
1/2 lb	Cooked shrimp (mini shrimp)
8 oz	Coconut milk
Dash	Sugar
1/2 cup	Hot water

Chef's Notes:
Serve with white rice, any fish and/or meat dish, french beans, atjar biet (Beet Salad) and/or cucumber.

❀ Using wok set on medium heat, sauté the red chilies, garlic, scallions, shrimp paste, tamarind and salt in butter until the onions are light brown Add the lemon grass, bay leaf, laos and lemon leaves. Stir. Add the cooked shrimp and simmer for 3 minutes. Add the coconut milk and sugar, stir. Add hot water, stir and let simmer 8-10 minutes, uncovered. Check water level often, adding additional hot water as necessary so that the sauce is plentiful.

Sambal Goreng Daging
HOT SAUTÉED MEAT

Chef's Notes:
The prep time for this dish is minimal, as the steak can be cooked the day before. The ease with which this dish can be made, in no way compromises its flavor. It is tasty either eaten by itself or when served with white rice, krupuk, and a salad.

4 tbsp	Virgin olive oil
2	Cloves garlic, minced
5	Scallions, minced
4	Red chilies, unseeded and minced
1/2 tsp	Sugar
1 tsp	Salt
1 tsp	Tamarind (asam)
1/2 tsp	Shrimp paste (trassi)
1/2 cup	Hot water
1 inch	Ginger root or 1 tsp powder (jahe)
2	Small bay leaves (daun salam)
1 lb	Cooked sirloin (or any left over steak), cut into long thin pieces

✹ Using a wok, sauté in 2 tbsp of oil the garlic, scallions and red chilies for 3 minutes. Strain and set aside. Combine the sugar, salt, tamarind and shrimp paste with 1/2 cup hot water. Using a separate pan, sauté this mixture, along with the ginger and bay leaves, in 2 tbsp of oil for 2-3 minutes. Add the meat, and the sautéed garlic, scallions and red chilies, stir. Add a dash of hot water and stir again. Return all of the ingredients to the wok, add a sprinkle of hot water and stir over medium heat until everything is heated through.

Sambal Goreng Timpi, II
HOT SAUTÉED SOY BEAN CAKE

Chef's Notes:
Serve this dish as an appetizer or side dish to anyone who likes their food spicy.

1	Timpi (soy bean flour cake)
4 tbsp	Virgin olive oil
2	Cloves garlic, minced
5	Scallions, minced
4	Red chilies, unseeded and minced
1/2 cup	Hot water
1/2 tsp	Sugar
1 tsp	Salt
1 tsp	Tamarind (asam)
1/2 tsp	Shrimp paste (trassi)
1 inch	Laos or 1 tsp powder
2	Small bay leaves (daun salam)

❈ To prepare, cut timpi into sections measuring 3 inches by 1 inch. Using wok, set on medium heat, cook the timpi slices in 2 tbsp of olive oil until light brown. Remove timpi and place on brown paper to drain. Using the same wok and oil, sauté the garlic, scallions and red chilies for 5 minutes. Drain and set aside on brown paper. Combine hot water with sugar, salt, tamarind and shrimp paste and using a small pan, sauté in 2 tbsp of olive oil for 1 minute. Add the laos and bay leaves and continue simmer for 2-3 minutes. Return all of the ingredients to the wok, add a sprinkle of hot water and simmer, over medium heat, until everything is heated through.

Sambal Goreng Telor
HOT SAUTÉED EGGS

Chef's Notes:
Serve with white rice, Sayur Menir, (spinach soup), krupuk, kecap or your choice of meat dish.

2	Red chilies, unseeded and minced
1 1/2	Cloves garlic, minced
3	Scallions, minced
1	Large green pepper, minced
2 tbsp	Butter
	Salt, to taste
4	Small lemon leaves (jerukpurut)
2	Small bay leaves (daon salam)
1 inch	Ginger root or 1 tsp powder (jahe)
1/4 tsp	Tamarind (asam)
1/4 tsp	Shrimp paste (trassi)
1/4 cup	Hot water
6	Hard boiled eggs, peeled and quartered
8 oz	Coconut milk
1/2 tsp	Sugar

❀ Using wok, set on medium heat, sauté the red chilies, garlic, scallions and green pepper in butter for 3 minutes. Add salt, lemon leaves, bay leaves, ginger, tamarind and shrimp paste. Stir. Add hot water, stir. Add eggs, coconut milk and sugar and let simmer, uncovered, for 8 minutes. Add additional hot water as necessary to maintain fluid level. When done, eggs should float in a sauce.

Please note that Kecap is also shown in photo.

Relishes and Sauces

Kecap Saus, I
KECAP SAUCE 1
(INDONESIAN SOY SAUCE)

Chef's Notes:
Always use a mortar and pestle to crush chilies.

5-6	Green chilies, minced
6 sprigs	Soup celery, minced
4 tbsp	Kecap manis (sweet soy sauce)
2 tbsp	Vinegar
1 tbsp	Sugar

❀ Remove seeds from peppers. Mince, crush and mash peppers. Combine with celery and set aside. In glass bowl, combine kecap, vinegar and sugar. Add peppers and celery. Cover and store until ready to use.

Kecap Saus, III
KECAP SAUCE III
(INDONESIAN SOY SAUCE)

Chef's Notes:
This version of the Kecap Sauce is the mildest and will suit most peoples' pallets.

2	Red chilies
2-3	Scallions
4 tbsp	Kecap
1/4 tsp	Salt
1 tsp	Sugar
	Juice of 1 lemon

❀ Remove seeds from peppers Mince peppers and scallions and set aside. In glass bowl, combine kecap, salt, sugar and lemon. Add peppers and scallions. Cover and store until ready to use.

Indonesia Saus Selada
INDONESIAN SALAD DRESSING

Chef's Notes:
Very refreshing when chilled and poured over sliced cucumbers.

4	Eggs, hardboiled
1/2 tsp	Salt
1/4 tsp	Pepper
Dash	Nutmeg
1 tbsp	Sugar
1 tsp	Brown mustard
1 tbsp	White vinegar
2 tbsp	Butter, melted
	Hot water

❋ Mince hard-boiled eggs and place in a mixing bowl. Add salt, pepper, nutmeg, sugar, mustard and vinegar, stir. Add melted butter, stir. Gradually add hot water, stirring constantly, until sauce is smooth.

Bawang Bombay Saus

ONION SAUCE

Chef's Notes:
This sauce goes well with Fried or Broiled Fish, pg 136, Mashed Potatoes, Cucumber or Beet Salad.

2	Large onions, finely minced
2 tbsp	Butter
1/4 tsp	Salt
1/4 tsp	Pepper
Dash	Nutmeg
1 tsp	Ginger powder (jahe)
1 tbsp	Kecap
2 tbsp	White vinegar
1 cup	Hot water
2 tbsp	Flour

❁ In wok, set on medium heat, sauté onions in butter until onions become light brown. Add salt, pepper, nutmeg, ginger and kecap. Stir. Add hot water and flour paste*. Continue simmering, stirring constantly, until sauce begins to thicken.

**To make flour paste, combine flour with enough cold water, mixing thoroughly to create a paste-like consistency.*

Kacang Saus

HOT PEANUT BUTTER SAUCE
FOR BEEF, PORK OR CHICKEN SATE

Chef's Notes:
This sauce can be served over any beef, pg 137,
pork or chicken sate. I prefer to reserve some
of the sauce to be served on the side.
This sauce can be made in any pot. However I
prefer to use a crock pot, letting all ingredients
simmer together for at least 1 hour. The longer
the sauce simmers, the tastier it is.

8 oz	Coconut milk (canned or fresh)
1/2 Jar	(about 14 ounces) Good quality Peanut butter
2	Red chilies, unseeded, minced and crushed
2	Scallions, minced and crushed
1-2	Cloves garlic, minced
3 tbsp	Kecap
1/2 tsp	Salt
1 tsp	Tamarind (asam), mixed w/enough water to form a paste (or can use tamarind jelly)
1 tsp	Java Sugar (gula jawa)
2-3	Lemon leaves (jeruk purut)
1/2 tsp	Shrimp paste (trassi)

✳ In crock pot, simmer coconut milk and peanut butter together, stirring often,. Add red chilies, scallions and garlic. Stir. Add Kecap, salt, tamarind, java sugar, lemon leaves and shrimp paste, until oil separates from peanut butter and forms a layer on top Stir and let simmer at least 10 minutes*.

See Chef's notes.

Jahe Saus
GINGER SAUCE

Chef's Notes:
This sauce is wonderful when used over any grilled fish. Also provides a nice addition to Nasi Goreng (fried rice).

2 cups	Water
2	Red chilies, unseeded and finely minced
1/4 tsp	Salt
1 tbsp	White vinegar
1/4 cup	Java sugar (gula jawa)
1 tsp	Ginger powder (jahe)
2 tbsp	Flour

❀ In medium-sized pan, bring water to a boil. Add red chilies, salt, vinegar, java sugar and ginger. Stir. Add flour paste*. Continue cooking until sauce begins to thicken.

*To make flour paste, combine flour with enough cold water, mixing thoroughly to create a paste-like consistency.

Rujak Saus
FRUIT SALAD SAUCES

Chef's Notes:
Any of these three sauces are a wonderful topping for sliced sour apples and/or cucumber slices. Each of these sauces varies greatly in ingredients but all offer a wonderful and unique flavor. Another added benefit is that they are extremely easy to prepare.

Sweet and Salty:

4 tbsp	Java sugar (gula jawa)
1/2 tsp	Worcestershire sauce
1 tbsp	Soy sauce
2 tbsp	Hot water

✹ Combine all ingredients, mixing thoroughly so that sauce is smooth and thin.

Chef's Notes:
This is a great dip for celery sticks, cucumbers and carrots.

Hot and Sweet:

1/2 tsp	Sambal Ulek (or can substitute with 1/2tsp dried, minced red chilies
8 tbsp	Java sugar (gula jawa)
1 tbsp	Tamarind water (tamarind mixed w/ water)
1 tbsp	Dutch Maggi soy sauce
1/8 tsp	Shrimp paste (optional)

✹ Combine all ingredients, mixing thoroughly so that sauce is smooth and thin.

Chef's Notes:
I generally serve this as a dip with celery and cucumber sticks before and with dinner. The men enjoy it with their beer.

Hot and Sour:

1/2 tsp	Sambal Ulek (or can substitute with 1/2 tsp dried, minced red chilies)
1 tbsp	White vinegar
1 tbsp	Petus U Dang (spicy fish paste)
2 tbsp	Hot Water

✹ Combine all ingredients, mixing thoroughly so that sauce is smooth and thin.

Kecap Ketimun Manis
CUCUMBERS IN SWEET KECAP SAUCE

Chef's Notes:
Once you have prepared this salad, let it chill in the refrigerator for a few hours before serving. It should be served cold.

1-2	Cucumbers
1/2 cup	Kecap manis
1/2 tsp	Salt
1/2 tbsp	Sugar
1/4 tsp	Pepper
1/4-1/2 tsp	Sambal Ulek (can substitute with dried and crushed red chilies)

❀ Rinse cucumber (do not peel). Cut cucumber length wise and remove seeds. Cut again, length wise and then again, until pieces measure approximately 1/2 inch by 4 inches long. Set aide. In a glass bowl, combine kecap, salt, sugar, pepper and sambal ulek. Add cucumber and stir well. Cover and store in refrigerator until ready to serve.

Sambal Ulek
CRUSHED CHILI RELISH

Chef's Notes:
This particular sambal, or relish, is used in many of the recipes in this book. You can either make it yourself and store it in the refrigerator or purchase it through Dutch or Indonesian import stores or through the mail order form printed in this book.

1 dozen	Red chilies
1/2 tsp	Shrimp paste (trassi)
1/2 tsp	Salt
1 tbsp	Tamarind juice (asam)

❋ Crush chilies, shrimp paste and salt together. Stir in tamarind juice, combining thoroughly. Place in a glass or ceramic container, cover and store in refrigerator until needed.

Relishes and Sauces

DESSERTS

The desserts of Indonesia are drastically different from what many of us are used to. They are mostly made from fruit and are much lighter than the typical cake and ice cream fare that we have become accustomed to.

The Indonesian people like "sweets", but prefer fruits which grow in abundance all over the island. Bananas and various citrus fruits grow in the back yard. There is no comparing the taste derived from a full sun-ripened banana with that which can be purchased in the supermarkets.

The desserts contained in this chapter are indicative of the Indonesian's ability to use what nature has provided. Not only are these desserts tasty and easy to prepare, but they are also much healthier than the usual cake and pie desserts.

Rempah Santan
FRIED COCONUT BALLS

Chef's Notes:
Serve these delicious coconut balls with satay, krupuk and the sambal of your choice.

1	Large lemon grass blade (sereh) or 1 tsp powder
1/2 tsp	Salt
1/4 tsp	Pepper
1	Small bay leaf (daun salam)
2	Lemon leaves (jeruk purut)
6 oz	Shredded coconut
1/2 tsp	Tamarind (asam)
1 1/2 oz	Coconut milk
1	Egg, beaten
2 tbsp	Butter or oil

✸ Finely mince lemon grass (or use powder) and place in mixing bowl. Add salt, pepper, bay leaf and lemon leaves. Crush everything together. Add coconut and stir. Add tamarind, coconut milk and egg. Using your hands, knead mixture well. Make small balls, 1 - 1 1/2 inches in diameter. Using a heated wok, fry coconut balls in butter or oil until fully cooked. (Should be a golden brown color when done).

Bloemkool Koekies
BERT'S SURPRISE
(CAULIFLOWER COOKIES)

Chef's Notes:
These cookies are so named due to my oldest son Bert's avid aversion to cauliflower. They can be used as a side dish to most any meal.

1/2 Head	Cauliflower
2	Eggs
1 oz	Coconut milk
1/2 tsp	Salt
1/4 tsp	Pepper
4 tbsp	Wheat flour
1	Clove garlic, finely minced
2	Scallions, finely minced
1-2 Sprigs	Soup celery, finely minced
1	Small leek, finely minced
1	Red chili, finely minced
	Butter or oil

❉ Cut cauliflower into 1/2 inch pieces. Set aside. Beat eggs with coconut milk, salt, pepper and wheat flour. Add garlic, scallions, celery, leek and red chili and stir well. Heat butter or oil in a wok. Using a soup ladle, drop by the 1/2 ladle and let cook until cookies are a golden brown.

Kwee Talam
BROWN AND WHITE CORN STARCH PUDDING

Chef's Notes:
This dessert is quick and simple, yet has the appearance of a restaurant dessert. It is a unique confection that is sure to impress your dinner guests. Whipped cream or vanilla sauce served on top will accent this fantastic dessert.

Brown Mixture:

3/4 cup	Corn starch
2 cups	Water
1 cup	Java sugar (gula jawa)
Dash	Salt
	Oil

White Mixture:

3/4 cup	Corn starch
2 cups	Water
1 cup	White sugar
3/4 cup	Coconut milk
Dash	Salt
3 inches	Daun pan dan (screw pine leaf)

❈ *To prepare brown mixture:* In small bowl, combine corn starch and some water to make a paste, set aside. In medium-sized pan, boil water and add sugar and salt. Stir and let boil until sugar dissolves. Remove from heat and pour sugar/salt mixture through a sieve. Combine sugar and salt with the corn starch paste and return to stove. Cook on medium heat, stirring often, until mixture begins to thicken and has a glossy appearance. Pour into greased glass or ceramic bowl. Set aside.

❈ *To prepare white mixture:* Combine corn starch with some water to make a paste, set aside. In medium-sized pan, boil water and add sugar, coconut milk, salt and daun pan dan and let simmer until mixture returns to a boil. Remove from heat, add corn starch mixture and then return to heat. Stir quickly and constantly until mixture becomes thick and has a glossy appearance. Remove from heat and pour on top of brown mixture. Let cool completely.

❈ *To serve:* Cut into small, pie-shaped pieces, (similar to pizza slices), and top with whipped cream or vanilla sauce.

Desserts

Kwee Bolah
POTATO SNOWBALL COOKIES

Chef's Notes:
These cookies make for an attractive dessert.
They are filling, delicious and nutritious.

10	Potatoes, peeled
2 tbsp	Wheat flour
2	Eggs
1/2 tsp	Salt
1 tbsp	Sugar to taste
1/2 tsp	Vanilla Extract
2 tbsp	Milk
	Oil
	Powdered sugar

❋ Boil and mash potatoes. Set aside and let cool completely. In mixing bowl, combine flour, eggs, salt, vanilla, sugar and milk. Add mashed potatoes. Combine thoroughly and make small balls about 1 inch in diameter. Heat oil in wok and drop the potato balls into the hot oil. Let cook until golden brown. Once they are completely cooked remove from oil and place on a wire rack. Sprinkle with powdered sugar.

Ongol - Ongol
COCONUT PUDDING

Chef's Notes:
This dish can be served as a dessert or as a cookie with a cup of tea.

3/4 cup	Corn starch
2 cups	Water
1/2	Vanilla bean, sliced open
7 oz	Java sugar (gula jawa)
Dash	Salt
	Oil (for greasing cookie sheet)
7 oz	Shredded coconut

✳ In small bowl, combine corn starch and some water to make a paste. Set aside. In medium-sized pan, bring 2 cups of water to a boil with vanilla bean, sugar and salt. Let cook, stirring often, until sugar completely dissolves. Remove from heat, add corn starch paste and then return to heat. Stir quickly and constantly until mixture becomes thick and has a glossy appearance. Pour mixture onto greased cookie sheet and let cool completely. Cut into 1-inch squares. Set aside. Combine coconut and salt and using a wok, simmer with 1 cup of water until water evaporates. Stir continuously so that coconut remains white. Cover pudding squares with the coconut mixture. Serve.

Jagung Koekies
CORN COOKIES

Chef's Notes:
These cookies are similar to corn fritters, but with more flavor and texture. They can be served as a side dish or as an accompaniment to tea.

1 sm. can	Whole kernel corn
4 tbsp	Wheat flour
1 oz	Coconut milk
1/2 tsp	Salt
1	Clove garlic, finely minced
2	Scallions, finely minced
2-3 Sprigs	Soup celery, finely minced
1	Red chili, unseeded and finely minced
1	Small leek
2	Eggs, beaten
	Butter or oil

✻ Boil corn in its own juice for 8-10 minutes. Drain and set aside. In mixing bowl combine flour, coconut milk and salt, making a paste. Add garlic, scallions, celery, red chili and leek. Add corn and eggs and mix thoroughly. Melt butter in wok set on medium heat. Using a soup ladle for measurement, drop batter into butter and cook until cookies become golden brown. Remove and let cool.

Pisang Koekies
BANANA COOKIES

6	Bananas, peeled
4 tbsp	Flour
2 tbsp	Sugar
2	Eggs
1/2 tsp	Cinnamon
1/2 cup	Milk
	Oil

Chef's Notes:
These cookies are as healthy as they are delicious. Your family is sure to gobble them up. They are also great for an afternoon treat.

* Cut banana into small bite-sized pieces. Set aside. In mixing bowl, combine flour, sugar, eggs, cinnamon and milk. Using wire whisk or electric mixer set on low, mix batter thoroughly. Stir in banana slices. Heat oil in wok set on medium heat. Using a soup ladle for measurement, drop batter into wok and cook until cookies become golden brown. Remove and let cool.

Agar - Agar
VANILLA GELATIN PUDDING

Chef's Notes:

Agar-Agar is a gelatin substance derived from seaweed. It is sold in most Asian import stores and in large supermarkets. I prefer to use mandarin orange slices in lieu of the mixed fruit.

1 1/2 pcs.	Clear gelatin (or 2 pkgs. of powder)
4 cups	Milk
1 tbsp	Sugar
1	Vanilla stick, cut lengthwise into shards (or 1 tsp vanilla extract)
1/2 can	Mixed fruit

❋ Boil gelatin pieces with some water until completely melted. (Or use powder, following package instructions.) In a separate pan, combine milk, sugar and vanilla stick. Stirring often, bring to a boil. Remove from heat. Add gelatin and stir until mixture begins to set. Rinse jello mold with cold water. Pour mixture into form and let cool in refrigerator until set, or overnight. To serve, arrange fruit on and around mold as decoration.

Rempejek Kacang
RICE FLOUR COOKIES WITH PEANUTS

Chef's Notes:
The unique blend of spices with the crunchiness of the peanuts makes for a delicious and unique snack.

7 oz	Rice flour
1 tsp	Salt
1/2 tsp	Pepper
1/2 tsp	Kencur powder (can use ginger powder as a substitute)
1 tsp	Coriander (ketumbar)
1/2 tsp	Cumin (jinten)
1	Scallion, minced
2	Cloves garlic, minced
8 oz	Coconut milk
2	Lemon leaves (jeruk purut)
9 oz	Peanuts
	Oil

❋ In mixing bowl, combine rice flour with salt, pepper, kencur, coriander and cumin. Add scallion, garlic and coconut milk. Mix thoroughly, making a paste. Crush lemon leaves and add to mixture. Stir in peanuts. Heat oil in wok. Using a ladle for measurement, make round flat cookies (like a thin hamburger patty) and cook in oil until golden brown.

THE RIGHT TOOLS FOR THE JOB

The preparation and cooking of the meals in this book will be more pleasurable if you have the right tools. There are two essential tools you must acquire - a wok and a mortar and pestle. I also suggest acquiring a rice steamer, although it is not essential.

Wok: Invest in a good one. I have had the same wok for 43 years. It is solid cast iron with a porcelain finish. They can be costly, but if you purchase a quality one, you will have it for life. I advise staying away from the no-stick or teflon-coated woks. They all eventually chip and then they are no good.

Mortar and Pestle: These are essential for crushing and/or mashing ingredients. And almost every recipe in this book calls for one or more ingredients to be crushed or mashed. It will also save you a lot of time in preparation.

Rice Steamer: The acquisition of a rice steamer is not essential, but it will make the preparation of certain foods, as well as rice, a bit easier. In lieu of a rice steamer you can use a bamboo or wicker basket, set over a pot of boiling water.

A WORD ABOUT SPICES

The Indonesian people live close to the land. They are in tune with nature and use nature to their advantage when cooking. The use of spices, a natural export of Indonesia, is without doubt, their forte. Necessity is the mother of invention and the Indonesian natives have invented, through thousands of years, a wonderful and exotic cuisine that is rich in flavor, spices and texture.

Unfortunately some of these spectacular spices can be difficult, if not impossible, to find anywhere outside of Indonesia. It is to our advantage that we live in a society that promotes world wide trading. However, they can still be difficult to locate. What follows is a list of the frequently used ingredients in the recipes of this book. I have tried to offer substitutions, (if any), where they can be purchased, and tips to making some of the ingredients yourself.

SPICES

Chili Peppers: The red chile is used in most every recipe, although green chilies are sometimes used. These can be found in almost any grocery store. They are small peppers, either dried or fresh and are intensely hot. I prefer to make minced dried red chilies myself. I do this by first cleaning and removing the seeds. (Use rubber gloves when cleaning any pepper). I then finely mince them and put them in a glass jar.

Coconut and Coconut Milk: Both of these are widely available in most grocery stores. You can, if you prefer, use fresh. By either grating a fresh coconut to make shredded coconut or to make fresh coconut milk, combine 1 cup of fresh, shredded coconut with 2 cups of luke warm water. Kneed by hand and then put through a sieve.

Coriander Seed: (ketumbar) This is a common spice that can be bought in most grocery stores.

Ginger: (jahe) This has become very popular in America and elsewhere - not only as an ingredient for cooking but also for medicinal purposes. It can be bought in almost any grocery store, either powdered or as a root. One inch grated is equivalent to one tsp., powder.

Gula Jawa: (java sugar) This can generally be bought only through import stores. However, you can make your own by combining 1/2 cup of premium molasses with 1 cup of dark brown sugar.

Indonesian Bay Leaf: (daun salam) It can be difficult to find this anywhere other than an Asian import store. Regular bay leaf can be used as a substitute.

Kecap: (Indonesian soy sauce) An all-purpose seasoning used in many recipes. It can be purchased in two varieties - sweet or salty. Kecap Manis, which is sweet, or Kecap Asin, which is salty. I suggest that you do not use Chinese soy sauce as a substitute, as it is generally too salty. You can purchase kecap through some Asian import stores or you can make your own by combining 1/2 cup of Gramma's unsulphured molasses with 1/2 cup of LaChoy soy sauce. Store in refrigerator.

Krupuk: Is a wafer - generally shrimp flavored, although other flavors are available. It can be purchased in most Asian import stores.

Laos: Is a root, indigenous to Indonesia. It can be purchased in some larger grocery stores and in most Asian import stores. It has a very pungent flavor and is difficult to simulate with a substitute. However, if absolutely necessary, substitutions can be made with the galanagal root or, as a last resort, the ginger root.

Lemon Grass: (sereh) Is a fairly common herb. It can be purchased in most grocery stores or you can grow your own. To substitute - 1 tsp. of lemon juice is equivalent to 1 blade of lemon grass.

Lemon Leaves: (jeruk purut) Can be bought in many grocery stores and in most Asian import stores, or, you can grow your own. You can substitute with lemon peel.

Shrimp Paste: (trassi) Can be purchased in most Asian import stores and in some larger grocery stores. There is no substitute.

Tamarind: (asam) Can be purchased from most Asian import stores and in some larger grocery stores. It comes in a whole, dried form, which you generally make into a paste by combining it with water. Or, you can purchase it in a jelly form, for which no alterations need be made. If using fresh, remove pit first, and finely mince before adding to recipe. I don't suggest using a substitute, but if necessary lime juice can be used.

One final note; altering or substituting the ingredients too much can easily alter the authenticity of the dish. Therefore, whenever possible, try to use the original ingredient, rather than the substitutions offered, so as to preserve the integrity of the recipe.

INDONESIAN-ENGLISH GLOSSARY

Indonesian	English	Indonesian	English
Adas	ManisAnise	Daun Salam	Indonesian Bay leaf
Asam	Tamarind	Djamoer-koeping	Chinese champignons
Ajam	Chicken	Dadar	Omelet
Ape	Apple	Daging	Meat
Arak	Rice wine	Dendeng	Dried spicy meat
Air	Water	Dragon	Tarragon
Asin	Salted	Dingin	Colt
Arang	Charcoal	Emping	Vegetable wafer
Agar-agar	Gelatin	Gula Jawa	Java sugar
Atjar	Salad	Gado-gado	Steamed vegetables w/peanut butter sauce
Babi	Pork		
Bahmi	Noodles	Goreng	Fry
Banteng	Buffalo	Gula	Sugar
Bakar	Grill	Gurami	Carp
Buah-kemiri	Almonds	Hati	Liver
Bawang-Bombay	Onions	Ikan	Fish
Bawang-merah	Scallions	Ikan-teri	Anchovy
Bawang-Putih	Garlic	Jeruk-sitrun	Lemon
Banjar	Mackerel	Jagung	Corn
Bayem	Spinach	Jahe	Ginger
Bebek	Duck	Jeruk	Citrus fruit
Beras	Uncooked rice	Jeruk purut	Lemon leaf
Biet	Beet	Jintan	Cumin
Bumbu	Spices	Kelapa	Coconut
Bumbu oseh-oseh	Meat seasoning	Kurma	Date
Bumbu Besegnek	Mixed spices	Kunyit	Turmeric
Cengkeh	Cloves	Kurkuma plant	Turmeric
Daun Bawang	Lettuce onion	Kacang tanam	Peanuts
Daun Jeruk purut	Lemon leaf	Kenari	Special almond
Daun	Leaf		

Indonesian	English	Indonesian	English
Kemirie	Candle Nut/Macadamia nut	Panggang	Roasting/grilling
Kentjur Zedoary	Powder	Pasar	Market
Ketumbar	Coriander	Pedes	Hot
Kucai	Leek	Prai	Leek
Kuning	Yellow	Panas	Warm food
Kembang-pala	Mace	Rebung	Bamboo shoots
Ketimun	Cucumber	Rebus	Boiled
Keluwek	Black-filled nut	Santan	Coconut milk
Kecap	Indonesian soy sauce	Sereh	Lemon grass
Kaju manis	Licorice stick wood	Sedep Malam	Dried mushrooms (night lily variety)
Kol	Type of cabbage		
Kubis	Type of cabbage	Sambal	Hot sauce
Kismis	Currant	Sapi	Beef
Krupuk	Wafers	Satay	Kabobs
Kemangi	Basil	Sayur	Vegetables
Limau	Lime	Serundeng	Spicy shredded coconut
Laos	Type of ginger root	Sop	Soup
Lombok	Red chili pepper	Selada-bawang	Salad onions
Laksa	Chinese vermicelli	Subi	Molasses
Lombok-rawit	Jalapeno pepper	Susu	Milk
Lada	Black pepper	Selada	Salad
Langkau	Halibut	Tahu	Tofu
Lobak	Black radish/ramenas	Taugeh	Bean sprouts
Makan	Eat	Timpi	Soy bean cake
Manis	Sweet	Temu-kunci	Moulo Powder
Mata Sapi	Fried egg (sunny side up)	Trassi	Shrimp paste
Nanas	Pineapple	Telur	Egg
Nasi	Rice	Terung	Eggplant
Pisang	Banana	Tomat	Tomato
Pala	Nutmeg	Tubuhan	Thyme
Peteh	Type of green bean	The	Tea
Pandan	Pine Nut	Udang	Shrimp

INDEX

Prop Credits

Stoneware by **The Lisa Howe Stoneware Collection**. Scottsdale, AZ. 85254 (see mail order sources) Pages 9-10, 23, 38, 46, 51, 67, 75, 78, 89, 97, 102, 107, 110, 122, 126, 131, 134, 135

Silverware by **Mexican Connection**. 7114 E.Sahuaro Drive. Scottsdale, AZ. 85254 Pages 75, 134

Batik Fabrics by **Gillyan Thorburn**. 1703 S. Carmelian Ave. Los Angeles, Ca. 90025. Pages 9-10, 134, 155

Mail Order Sources

Indonesian Spices
International Delights Inc.
7645 E. Evans Dr. Suite 6
Scottsdale, AZ. 85260

For a catalog please call:
Toll free 888-626-0836 ext.558

Stoneware
The Lisa Howe Stoneware Collection
7129 E. Mercer Lane. Scottsdale, AZ. 85254

For a catalog please call 1-800-996-6769